BEYOND BABY STEPS

BEYOND BABY STEPS

A SCIENCE-BASED APPROACH TO MODERN-DAY PARENTING

LAHAR BHATNAGAR SINGH

HAY HOUSE INDIA
New Delhi • London • Sydney
Carlsbad, California • New York City

Hay House Publishers (India) Pvt Ltd,
Muskaan Complex, Plot No. 3, B-2, Vasant Kunj, New Delhi 110 070, India
Hay House LLC, P.O. Box 5100, Carlsbad, CA 92018-5100, USA
Hay House UK Ltd, The Sixth Floor, Watson House, 54 Baker Street, London W1U 7BU, UK
Hay House Australia Publishing Pty Ltd, 18/36 Ralph St., Alexandria NSW 2015, Australia

Email: contact@hayhouse.co.in
www.hayhouse.co.in

10 9 8 7 6 5 4 3 2 1
First Hay House India Edition, 2024

ISBN 978-81-19554-70-6
ISBN 978-81-19554-39-3 (Ebook)

Printed at Replika Press

MIX
Paper | Supporting responsible forestry
FSC™ C016779

To,
Maninder

For being my constant support and anchor
and preventing me from turning into Momzilla!

Contents

Introduction

A 5-year-old lives on one roti all day and refuses to eat without watching Peppa Pig on YouTube. A classmate's vacation to a foreign destination sparks a similar request from your child. While your kid's best friend flaunts the latest iPhone, you try to maintain a no-phone policy until the age of 14. A 10-year-old boy faces teasing from his friends for not having kissed a girl yet. Your daughter, influenced by societal standards, spends excessive time in front of the mirror, disliking her broad jaw due to its impact on her selfies.

These are some of the unique parenting challenges that have emerged in the millennium era. But an important question to consider here is how we, as parents and guardians, even start to understand the psychological and emotional turmoil our children go through when we ourselves did not face such high pressure, competitive environments, and demands of an internet-dominated world during our upbringing? And despite recognising the necessity of passing on our life lessons and experiences to our children, the challenge arises when it comes to providing guidance and counsel on issues we haven't navigated ourselves. Thankfully a lot of research and studies are being conducted on issues of new-age parenting. Therefore, a practical approach to addressing these challenges would involve first understanding the insights provided by scientific inquiry and research.

Years of research conducted by child psychologists, neuroscientists, and anthropologists hold invaluable insights that every parent could benefit from. By delving into these findings, mothers can gain a deeper understanding of child development, cognitive processes, and social dynamics, empowering them to make informed decisions and cultivate nurturing environments for their children to thrive. Hence, the most effective approach involves blending scientific research with practicality and firsthand experience. This is exactly what this book aims to do. Leveraging my background in neuroscience and the practical wisdom gained from raising two wonderful millennial kids and my profession as a parenting coach, I aim to share intriguing scientific insights relevant to parenting and how to translate those findings into simple household hacks. You can use this book as a reference, guide, pocketbook, friend, therapist, or even a comforting pillow to snuggle with at night that is sure to offer reassurance, peace, and a positive perspective to enhance your parenting journey.

Before you dive into the world of scientific parenting, let me leave you with one little anecdote. I like to emphasise to anyone who comes to me for parental guidance that for parenting to be effective, our parenting source should be our kids and not us. What this means is that we let our kids guide us in how they need to be raised instead of imposing our ideas and knowledge on them. Don't worry if this concept sounds vague right now. We will extrapolate in detail all the insights and tips in the following chapters and soon, you may find yourself writing to me about how this small shift in perspective has opened doors to joyful parenting in your life.

As a concluding note, I hope you will enjoy reading the book as much as I enjoyed penning it down.

Now let's begin our parenting journey.

What Is Nirvana-Ma?

My parenting resource is called Nirvana-Ma. The word 'nirvana' means an idyllic state of mind where one experiences perfect peace and happiness and the word 'ma' is a Sanskrit term for mother and an expression used for mother across many languages and cultures. However, in the word Nirvana-Ma, the suffix of 'ma' can refer to any caregiver who aids in the child's development, be it a mother, a father, grandparents, etc. Thus, the Nirvana-Ma philosophies are not restricted to only the mother; they can be and should be embraced and practised by the entire family involved in nurturing a child.

The fundamental principle of Nirvana-Ma centres on the idea that the roots of adults' personalities trace back to their upbringing. How individuals were nurtured and raised not only shapes their current selves but also influences how they react and treat others. This underscores the significance of the Nirvana-Ma concept, emphasising the need for well-informed, stress-free, and liberated nurturing.

With a background in neuroscience and brain development, I have observed the transformative power of simple scientific principles. Therefore, all the models developed at Nirvana-Ma have three key pillars:

1. They are scientific.
2. They are simple.
3. They are sustainable.

This implies that the parenting models, workshops, and tips at Nirvana-Ma are based on scientifically sound models of brain anatomy and evolution. Despite their scientific foundation, they remain simple, powerful, and universally applicable, transcending differences in household environments, culture, customs, financial status, etc. Simply put, scientific parenting, as advocated by Nirvana-Ma, essentially means 'parenting as nature intends.'

To know more about the intricacies of scientific parenting and Nirvana-Ma, you can write to me at nirvanamaa@gmail.com.

Chapter 1

Screen Time

One of the biggest technological advancements of the 20th century is the dawn of the internet and electronic gadgets. The internet was envisioned as a tool that would bring the world into the palm of our hand, give us an open access to a sea of knowledge, and connect us to people from all over the globe at the click of a button. While it has certainly achieved that, it has also brought with it some challenges.

Post-millennial kids, born after 1995, practically have Wi-Fi gadgets at their fingertips from the moment they enter the world. Unlike the older generation, which had limited TV viewing hours for entertainment, Gen Z has access to millions of hours of on-demand content. Add to that social media which consumes endless hours of their day. As a result, an entire generation of toddlers, teens, and young adults treats mobile phones or tablets as if they were extended appendages.

Now, the question arises: Why is screen addiction such a significant problem? How does it surpass the challenges posed by cable TV, which was a major parenting concern in the 80s? Are the impacts of excessive screen time truly substantial enough to demand a significant portion of our parenting efforts? Before delving into a detailed exploration of these queries, let's initially examine the primary physical and non-physical challenges arising from screen addiction.

I. Physical Challenges

1. ADHD (Attention Deficit Hyperactivity Disorder)

If you had visited the Seattle Children's Research Institute in 2018, you would have encountered a surprising sight: small TV lounges where mice were engrossed in watching videos. Dr Dimitri Christakis, the institute's director, conducted a crucial experiment exposing young mice, aged 10 to 52 days, to six hours of daily TV viewing. The media they watched mimicked the pace, lighting, and auditory stimulation of regular cartoons viewed by human kids. Subsequently, the mice underwent standard behavioural tests, evaluating brain hyperactivity and attention levels. The results showed a clear statistical correlation between TV viewing in mice and issues like hyperactivity, lower attention spans, and increased boredom.

This study sheds light on the significant rise in conditions like ADHD (attention deficit hyperactivity disorder) in young kids today. Excessive screen time appears to contribute to the development of hyperactive preteens, easily bored toddlers, and children with short attention spans. In simpler terms, their exposure to fast-paced, colourful, and exciting screen content makes real-life experiences less stimulating. Consequently, they struggle with boredom, have difficulty paying attention, and find it challenging to adjust to reality. They become so entangled with screens that persuading them to step outside and play requires a comprehensive psychological rewiring strategy.

2. Childhood Obesity

Another growing global concern is the alarming surge in childhood obesity. Scientific studies conducted in both urban and rural areas of India, as well as in the West, highlight two primary reasons for the connection between obesity and screen time. Firstly, there's the excessive exposure to food advertising, primarily showcasing unhealthy junk food, while engaging with TV, YouTube videos, or online media. Consequently, digital kids experience a significant uptake in the consumption of fried, sugary, and unhealthy food items. Parents of toddlers post-2010 can attest to the fact that children often develop intense cravings for something they have seen on TV or their iPads, and unfortunately, commercials for healthier options like broccoli or spinach are not as prevalent. Moreover, it's challenging to enjoy a wholesome meal of dal, sabzi, or chicken curry while engrossed in screen time, leading to a preference for finger foods like chips, soda, or salami sandwiches.

The second reason connecting child obesity to screen time is the noticeable reduction in sleep. Prolonged hours of media exposure and chatting deprive toddlers and teens of essential sleep. Numerous studies have linked sleep and obesity, emphasising the significance of 8-9 hours of uninterrupted sleep for optimal weight management. However, the Digi Gen isn't meeting these sleep recommendations, which coupled with unhealthy eating habits contribute to India now having the second-highest number of obese kids globally, with a reported 14.4 million cases.

It is evident that reduced physical activity and outdoor play due to excessive screen time are taking a toll on the physical health of children. Furthermore, studies have shown decreased bone density and growth among young kids and teenagers spending more time on screens than engaging in outdoor activities.

3. **Maladaptive Decision-Making**

   In 2012, Dr Lin and Dr Zhou published concerning results from their research. Neuroimaging studies on internet-addicted teens revealed significant alterations in brain structure. Previously established in cocaine and substance addicts, a decrease in white matter in the anterior cingulate cortex and corpus callosum was also observed in the brains of screen-addicted teenagers. These brain regions play a critical role in emotional processing and decision-making. Consequently, the unrestricted use of screen time in toddlers and kids, whose developing brains undergo neural pruning based on external stimuli, significantly raises the likelihood of maladaptive decision-making in the future.

4. **Depression and Anxiety**

   A more recent study in San Diego focused on examining 40,000 American children aged 2-17 years. The findings directly linked prolonged screen time to an increased incidence of depression and anxiety in children. Those who spent 7 hours or more in front of screens each day were significantly more prone to depression, anxiety, and overall low well-being. To put this into perspective, an article in *India Today* magazine estimated in 2015 that teenagers spend a staggering 9 hours on screens every day! Additionally, traditional remedies for stress, anxiety, depression, and various psychological disorders, such as exercise and meditation, find little traction among the digital generation which is engrossed in screens all day. This, in turn, creates a distressing and self-perpetuating cycle.

5. **Eye Health Complications**

   Screens also contribute to eye strain and dryness, leading to a significant increase in near-sightedness cases among young children. Ophthalmologists advise taking breaks of about a minute every hour spent on the screen and utilizing options such as the blue light filter to mitigate these effects. 'I prefer to teach kids better habits, instead of supplying them a crutch like reading glasses to enable them to consume even more media,' expressed K. David Epley, MD and clinical spokesperson for the American Academy of Ophthalmology. 'If you run too far and your legs start hurting, you stop. Likewise, if you have been reading too long or watching videos too long, and your eyes start hurting, you should stop.' For practical purposes, optometrists recommend the 20-20-20 rule: every 20 minutes, look away from the screen for 20 seconds and focus on something 20 feet away. While it may be challenging to establish this habit (for both kids and adults alike), it is important to preserve your precious eyes.

6. **Disrupted Circadian Rhythm**

   The list of physical issues doesn't stop here. Anyone becoming a parent in the new millennium will confirm that the most significant parenting stress is the disrupted circadian rhythm kids face today. The common mom rant these days is, 'They stay up till 2 a.m. watching Netflix or logged into Snapchat and then sleep till noon!' The war against the natural body clock has reached epidemic levels. The blue light from screens tricks the brain into believing it is still daylight, eventually disrupting the entire body clock, or circadian rhythm. If one watches screens late in the evening, the body thinks it is still daytime and does not release melatonin. Melatonin is a chemical that signals the body that it is getting dark, and sleep time is near. Melatonin helps induce sleepiness and promotes continuous sleep. It's no wonder insomnia and difficulty sleeping are significant problems among teens and adults alike! While you might calculate that your child is sleeping for 10 hours, it's not only about the hours but also when these hours are accumulated. So, sleeping at 1 a.m. and getting up at 11 a.m. shouldn't give you the mental reassurance that your teen is getting the recommended 10 hours of sleep.

II. Non-Physical Challenges

1. Lack of Empathy

When it comes to non-physical aspects, a crucial point emphasised in Dr Borba's book, *Unselfie,* delves into the diminishing empathy observed among young kids and teenagers. In a podcast interview, Dr Borba said, 'Our children became very plugged in around the year 2000. It's very hard to be empathetic and feel for another human being if you can't read another person's emotions. You don't learn emotional literacy facing a screen. You don't learn emotional literacy with emojis.'

But why is empathy important? Evolutionarily, empathy is the single trait that sets us apart from animals. Our increased brain capacity led us to be empathetic. Empathy is the strongest trait that helped humans to set up a society, work together, and benefit from each other. An empathetic person is not only likely to be a better person but also makes for a much better leader and corporate citizen. A Harvard Business review stated that top companies hire people with higher EQ (emotional quotient) than those with higher IQ. Empathy makes up a huge part of our emotional quotient. So, if you want to raise a child who bags that million-dollar pay package in the future, make sure that screen time is limited, and empathy is high!

2. Impacts Capability of Delayed Gratification

Another essential skill is the ability to practice delayed gratification. The renowned Stanford Marshmallow Experiment in 1972, led by psychologist Walter Mischel, involved offering a child a choice between a small reward immediately or two small rewards if they waited for approximately 15 minutes. The reward was either a marshmallow or a pretzel stick, based on the child's preference. Subsequent studies found that children who could wait longer for preferred rewards tended to have better life outcomes, as indicated by SAT scores, educational attainment, BMI, and other measures. Regrettably, in today's world of instant gratification, the ability to wait for 15 minutes for a reward is a rare skill among most kids.

I recall eagerly anticipating Sundays for my favourite show, *Jungle Book*, and the whole week was filled with excitement. When Sunday finally arrived, the surreal excitement I felt still gives me goosebumps today. Unfortunately, the current generation struggles with the concept of 'waiting it out.' Consequently, they are more likely to be impatient, less empathetic, inflexible, and, most unfortunately, unwilling to experience boredom.

3. Alienation

Contrary to its intended purpose, the internet is fostering isolation. Numerous studies highlight how the internet and social media contribute to clinical addiction. Tragically, reports of teenage depression or even suicides stemming from a lack of social media 'likes' reflect the harsh reality of modern society. Further complicating the matter is the fact that while drug addiction can be addressed by eliminating drugs from an individual's life, screen addiction involves ubiquitous mobile phones or gadgets in households. This makes effective screen management a significant challenge for every family.

4. Psychiatric Disorders

In the West, there is a growing acknowledgement that 'screen addiction' may soon become a subject of psychiatric studies. It exhibits characteristics typical of psychiatric disorders—disrupting social life, children prioritising screens over real social interactions, bans on screens causing emotional upheaval, and children using social media as an escape from societal pressures or personal problems. Moreover, most businesses, regardless of size, profit from online advertising, incentivising them to encourage prolonged online engagement. This pervasive issue seldom receives attention from media platforms, organizations, or NGOs, as it directly impacts their revenue streams. As a result, the battle against excessive screen time largely falls on the shoulders of parents.

Effective Strategies for Parents

Considering the array of challenges posed by screen addiction, is there any hope to overcome these obstacles? The answer is a resounding yes! However, it is crucial to recognise that balance is the key. Completely isolating your child from the screen is neither wise nor practical. Instead, you need to monitor both the time spent and the content your child engages with on the screen. Unfortunately, as early as age 3, many parents find themselves grappling with ways to curtail their child's screen time and manage the associated tantrums.

In the following pages, I will share a few tips for reducing screen time addiction in your child's life. However, my aim is to empower you to generate even more strategies based on your child and home environment. To achieve this, we first need to grasp the fundamental approach that underlies all the practical tips I will provide.

1. Attack the Real Problem

Often, we adopt a narrow and myopic perspective when it comes to understanding a child's challenges. We tend to label something as a problem based on a doctor's opinion, advice from fellow parents, or an advertisement featuring a person in a white coat with a stethoscope. In many cases, we haven't delved into the why behind a particular issue. Without understanding the why, addressing the 'how to get rid of it' aspect becomes challenging.

Consider screen time as an example. Some parents take pride in proclaiming that their child is not allowed even a minute of screen time. It is important to note that the internet itself is not inherently evil; it is the misuse that poses a problem. The internet offers a vast array of knowledge, but we often succumb to its less constructive aspects. Instead of vilifying the internet, we should focus on teaching our kids to use it responsibly. For instance, my daughter learned the English language by watching Peppa Pig on YouTube, and now she is attempting to learn Spanish through Dora. Clearly, the internet has positive applications as well.

2. Be Practical

Practicality is the cornerstone of resolving any social problem. While the ideal scenario would involve abandoning social media, engaging in face-to-face conversations, making friends, enjoying nature walks, and reading books, convincing a child to abruptly adopt a different approach, especially when their peers are deeply engrossed in games and social media can be challenging. Therefore, it is crucial to propose reforms that are not only idealistic but also practical in both approach and execution.

Screen addiction, academic struggles, or aversions were not inherent traits your child was born with; they developed gradually over time. To reverse these patterns, it is essential to take gradual steps backwards. Consider reducing screen time by 15 minutes each week, slowly working towards the recommended 60-120 minutes per day of screen usage. This incremental approach can be more effective and sustainable.

3. **It's Never Too Late**

   Don't be in a hurry to hang your gloves yet. Even if you are dealing with a pre-teen or a teenager, it's not a lost cause. You can still apply the tips and techniques outlined in this book to overcome the challenges you or your child might be facing. While the adage 'earlier, the better' holds true, it doesn't imply that a teenager's mom can't become a Nirvana-Ma. It might require more time and concerted efforts compared to dealing with a toddler, but success is assured in the end. Remember, as long as there is willingness and commitment, positive changes are always within reach.

4. **Don't Panic**

   If there were a defining characteristic for parents worldwide, it would undoubtedly be panic. All parents seem to be in a perpetual state of panic. Unfortunately, nothing transmits faster from you to a child than panic and anxiety. Children these days are exceptionally anxious, experiencing more stress than we did at their age. This heightened stress is a direct result of witnessing anxious, panicked, and fearful parenting around them all the time. Everything becomes a battle, a race, or a red flag!

I urge you to shed that fear cloak, dear parents, and embrace parenting with a calmer, mellower approach. Parenting is an ongoing learning process and should not be laden with stress or anxiety.

5. **Affirmative Instead of Authoritative**

   GenZ individuals don't respond well to authority. Phrases like 'I am your parent. I know better.' or 'I told you to do so!' won't resonate with your child. It is essential to employ a friendly and constructive approach. A friendly approach doesn't equate to spoiling the child. There is a prevalent notion that parents should instil fear and authority to prevent their child from becoming spoiled. The sentiment 'Tumhare pyaar ne hi bigaada hai' (Your love has spoilt him/her) is often echoed, and I strongly disagree. Love, in itself, can never spoil anyone; it is the interpretation of love that does. If you believe that showering your child with luxuries and toys is love, you are likely to spoil them. The child may be content with just three toys but dedicating 30 minutes a day to play with those toys is what matters. Giving in to a crying child because you can't bear to see them cry is not love. A firm yet polite approach is love, not succumbing to every demand. Use your negatives sparingly, but when you say no, stick to it. Regardless of how much your child protests or pleads, there is no need to yell or scream. Simply stand your ground. That is love.

6. **Identify Time Points**

   Allowing screen time during meals has become a common practice for many families, with around 90 per cent of kids being permitted to watch TV or use devices while eating. If you find yourself in this category, it doesn't necessarily mean you're a bad parent; it is simply a widespread habit. However, it is important to recognise the potential drawbacks and consider minimising screen time during these crucial moments in your child's day. By making meals, study sessions, and bedtime screen-free zones, you can help promote healthier habits and foster better focus and engagement in other activities.

Practical Tips for Managing Screen Time

1. **Use a Timer or Screen Management Apps**

   Completely isolating your child from screens isn't the ideal solution. The WHO recommends specific screen times for different age groups:

   i. 0-2 years: No screens
   ii. 2-5 years: 1 hour daily
   iii. 5-adult: 2 hours daily

   If your child exceeds these recommendations, there is no need to panic. Gradually work towards approaching the recommended time. A helpful starting point is to set a timer when they begin screen time. Consider exploring various 'screen management apps' available for free. These apps allow you to monitor screen usage and set timers to automatically disable Wi-Fi after a certain duration. So, why not use technology to combat technology!

2. **Set Specific Time Slots for Screen Usage**

   Rather than outright telling a child to avoid screens, it's more effective to specify designated times for screen use.

Reward them when they adhere to their timetable. Create a schedule that includes allocated screen time, dividing the total recommended daily duration into 2 or 3 slots and providing multiple screen options throughout the day. This approach makes screen time a regulated and rewarding part of their routine.

3. **Prepare Your Child for Screen Exposure at Parties**

   Most children can be found glued to their mobile phones during social gatherings or family events, making it challenging to steer them away from screens. However, a simple strategy to combat excessive screen time is to prepare your child beforehand. By discussing the upcoming event with your child a day prior, you can express your concerns about screen-time balance and outline your expectations for the occasion. Share stories about the fun activities and engaging opportunities that await them at the party or picnic, emphasising the enjoyment to be had beyond screens. This approach helps instil a positive mindset and encourages your child to participate in the event without relying solely on electronic devices.

4. **Monitor Your Child's Online Activity**

   Whenever your child is online, ensure that the screen is logged in from your account for later history checking. It's crucial not only to monitor the time spent online but also to supervise the content your child watches. Occasionally, children may access age-inappropriate content through the suggested video links.

5. **Have a Screen-Free Day**

   This one is specially for the adults in the house. Similar to occasional fasting to detox our bodies, incorporating a digital detox day is essential to reset our tired brains and rediscover the other pleasures in life. It is equally important for adults to actively participate in the screen-free day. Setting a good example is one of the most effective ways to teach valuable lessons. By committing to a weekly screen detox, not only will you lead by example, but you will also reap the benefits of a healthier relationship with technology, which your brain will undoubtedly appreciate.

6. **Encourage Your Child to Explore a Diverse Range of Content**

   Many parents prioritise educational content, but let's be honest—when was the last time you watched NatGeo or Discovery channel for knowledge? We primarily use media for entertainment, and our kids are no different. While kids naturally enjoy learning, it is okay to let them indulge in a few minutes of pure senseless entertainment via screens. However, it is essential to steer clear of games involving violence, nudity, and objectionable language.

7. **Encourage Your Child to Create Short Videos**

   Tap into the creative possibilities offered by technology for your child. Encourage them to explore their creativity by capturing videos and moments without the immediate pressure to share them online. This allows them to enjoy the process of creation without the distractions of social media or the internet. Keep in mind that while you want your children to be comfortable with technology, you don't want them to become overly dependent or addicted to it.

8. **Discuss Internet Security with Your Child Regularly**

   It is our responsibility to shield our kids from internet threats. Don't assume everyone is innocent online. Ensure toddlers and pre-teens don't have access to chat or messenger apps where unknown profiles can contact them. Install kid-friendly apps like YouTube Kids for safety.

9. **Nature Walks Beat Screen Time**

   Embracing nature's wonders offers endless opportunities for your child's growth and development. Activities like strolling in the park, playing soccer with friends, or simply enjoying a walk outdoors can ignite their curiosity and imagination. Taking nature walks together not only offers a refreshing break from screens but also encourages observation and inquiry. For instance, cloud-gazing, a beloved childhood pastime, prompts children to identify shapes and creatures in the clouds, nurturing creativity and fostering cherished memories beyond the digital world. Remember the joy of envisioning lions and dragons in the clouds? It is moments like these that fuel creativity and imagination, leaving a lasting impact on young minds.

10. **Promote Occasional Moments of Idleness**

   Introduce a 5-minute 'boredom break' into your child's daily routine. In today's digital age, where constant stimulation is the norm, the art of being bored is often overlooked. By incorporating this brief period of 'Bored Time,' you can teach your child the value of delayed gratification and encourage them to embrace moments of quiet reflection. Not only does it provide a chance for the brain to reset and recharge, but it also fosters creativity and imagination.

11. Family Bonding through Board Games

Explore the joy of playing classic board games like Ludo, Snakes and Ladders, and Chess with your child. These timeless games not only provide entertainment but also create memorable family moments. Share anecdotes from your own childhood experiences of playing these games, adding a personal touch to the family bonding session.

12. Badge of Distinction

Encourage your child to craft quirky badges as a reward for opting out of screen time and engaging in alternative activities. Create badges with empowering messages like 'Screen warrior' or 'I beat the screen!' to celebrate moments when your child successfully limits screen time. Allow your child to proudly display these badges to friends, sparking a potential competition among kids to reduce screen time. It's a win-win for everyone.

Chapter 2

TEMPER TANTRUMS

I once came across a highly creative YouTube commercial featuring a toddler throwing a tantrum in a grocery store about a candy which left the exasperated dad contemplating whether he should have used a condom a few years back! While it was hilariously creative, parents dealing with tantrum-throwing children might not find it as amusing.

Until recently, temper, anger, and tantrums were not extensively studied in child behaviour. However, a 2012 study by Daniels et al, published in the *Journal of American Academy of Nurse Practitioners,* revealed that the primary reason parents sought counselling was their child's temper and anger. Dealing with toddler tantrums is crucial as it lays the foundation for the rules of discipline and the family's overall attitude toward it. Mishandling or mismanaging tantrums can jeopardise the goal of raising a disciplined, level-headed child. In the following sections, we will unravel the intricacies of tantrums in children and discuss strategies for more effective management.

Tantrums in Children

In the renowned book, *Children's Needs,* Mc Curly et al highlighted that temper tantrums are frequent in 18-60 month-old toddlers. In another correlation study, paediatric behaviour researchers Dr Potegal and Dr Davidson documented and analysed the emotional and physical aspects of childhood tantrums. Their studies indicate that normal meltdown episodes typically last around 3 minutes on average and involve typical tantrum behaviours like whimpering, screaming, throwing hands and legs, pushing, biting, and even holding of breath.

While this information is reassuring as it shows that tantrums are common in all households, it is important to understand what a child's developing brain conveys through tantrums and why it becomes the preferred outlet for releasing latent energy. Researchers Green and Potegal turned every parent's nightmare into an organised study with streamlined data. They discovered that different tantrum sounds had distinct audio signatures, offering insights into the rhythm of tantrums. Therefore, recognising when a child transitions from anger to sadness during a tantrum can empower parents to intervene effectively. Tantrums, on average, last three minutes and cover a wide spectrum of sounds. Green and Potegal found that sad sounds consistently occurred throughout tantrums, interspersed with sharp peaks of yelling and screaming representing anger. The key to ending a tantrum quickly, according to Potegal, is navigating the peaks of anger. Once the child moves past the anger, what remains is sadness, prompting the child to seek comfort. Understanding this emotional progression equips parents with valuable tools for managing tantrums.

Now let's delve deeper by looking at a scenario which every parent can relate to. Your toddler's tantrum is unfolding with a burst of anger. The child turns red, screams, hits, and exhibits high-pitched crying. After a few minutes (assuming you haven't given in), the tantrum transitions into a different phase marked by sad crying, whimpering, and tired body language. This shift is crucial, and if you haven't noticed it in your child's tantrums, pay attention during the next episode.

However, recognising this transition is just step 2, according to most parents. Comforting or managing the tantrum comes later. When facing the dreaded emotional meltdown, which studies suggest lasts an average of three minutes, many toddler parents feel it lasts an eternity. Unfortunately, most of us are guilty of not always reacting in the most cordial manner during those three minutes. Incidents of yelling at, shaking, or even hitting the child may occur in a desperate attempt to end the tantrum. Some parents even succumb to the tantrum's demands, purchasing the triggering toy or candy—a tactic akin to a total death trap! And while some progressive parents advocate phrases like 'Don't be angry' or 'Use your words instead of cries,' they also acknowledge that, kind as these words may be, they often prove ineffective in stopping a tantrum. It is a challenging scenario familiar to many parents navigating the tumultuous waters of toddlerhood.

So, what should you do when a tantrum is in full swing? The scientifically-backed answer might surprise you which is—do nothing! Grover et al, contributors to the 2008 book, *Berkowitz Paediatric Care*, shed light on explaining, managing, and handling toddler tantrums. Their studies unequivocally state that maintaining calmness and refraining from taking any action is the most effective technique when a child is in the throes of a meltdown. If you sense the fiery volcano of anger erupting within you, it is even advisable to leave the room or space of the tantrum to prevent unleashing your heated frustration on your little one.

But is 'doing nothing' truly scientific advice? To comprehend this, we need a basic understanding of the human brain and its functioning. Our brain can be likened to a three-scoop ice cream cone. Picture the cone as your brain stem; the structure linking your brain to the spine. Now, envision placing the first scoop directly on the cone. This initial scoop is the reptilian brain. Add another scoop on top of the first one, the limbic brain, which constitutes the second layer. The third scoop represents the topmost layer of the brain, the neocortex, including the prefrontal lobes. The reptilian brain, primarily responsible for survival, governs the well-known flight, fight, or freeze instinct. This brain reacts to life-threatening situations and gets activated in the face of danger. For example, when confronted with a peril like an approaching tiger, humans instinctively choose flight (running away), fight (confronting the threat), or freeze (remaining still, hoping to evade detection). While this adrenalin-induced flight-fight-freeze response is beneficial for survival, it comes at the cost of compromised logic and reasoning. Evolutionarily, it ensures immediate action without pausing for analysis which is essential for survival when faced with a predatory threat like a hungry tiger. But in our modern context, we no longer grapple with the daily caveman challenges of fighting tigers. However, our brain wiring still mirrors that of a caveman. In other words, when the brain perceives something as a threat, it defaults to survival mode, temporarily suspending input from the reason and logic centres of the neocortex.

For children, the logic centre (neocortex) is still developing. A telling example is their fear of a caged tiger's roar, despite reassurances from their parents. This fear stems from the underdeveloped prefrontal cortex (PFC), responsible for logical thinking. Moreover, for the developing brain of a young child, modern-day threats can range from feeling uncomfortably warm due to wearing too many sweaters, wanting a shiny toy in the mall denied by parents, or accepting candy from a stranger. All these scenarios present potential dangers that trigger the brain's survival mode.

In summary, we can see that the main culprit behind a child's hissy fit is the reptilian brain, which gets activated when the child's desire is met with resistance, triggering the 'need, need, need' response. Denial of the desired object translates to a perceived threat, invoking the reptilian brain's fight, fright, or freeze reaction which is manifested through physical outbursts, screams, and even breath-holding.

Additionally, children, who are unburdened by social norms, unabashedly display tantrums. Their reptilian brain operates independently of societal judgements, indifferent to onlookers or wardrobe malfunctions. The child's sole focus is ensuring parents grasp their discontent with unfolding events. In *Idiot Brain,* Dr Dean Burnett eloquently links toddler tantrums to brain anatomy and psychology. From an evolutionary perspective, tantrums serve as a mechanism for a child to garner maximum attention within a group or community. The ensuing flailing and wailing, biologically imperative, can both ward off predators and summon adult assistance.

Understanding brain anatomy reveals the inefficacy of logic-centred directives like 'Use your words' or 'Don't be angry during tantrums.' Toddlers' underdeveloped logic centre renders logical solutions ineffective and redundant. Moreover, a child's speech centre is still learning, with word formation peaking around 24-36 months. Expecting a toddler to articulate complex emotions, like jealousy, is similar to speaking Mandarin to an unfamiliar audience. Recognising these developmental milestones reinforces the wisdom of allowing 3-10 minutes of reptilian brain dominance during tantrums.

Hence, embracing 'doing nothing' emerges as sound scientific advice for managing toddler tantrums. It isn't fostering indiscipline but granting the child a brief release for pent-up emotions, a universally warranted reprieve. But while 'doing nothing' dominates the 'to-do' list for tantrum control, a crucial 'do-not' checklist emerges as well for managing tantrums positively, This list has been outlined below:

1. Avoid telling the child to stop misbehaving due to onlookers.
2. Refrain from attempting to bribe with sweets or candy.
3. Never give in to the tantrum after initially saying no.
4. Avoid hugging the child if unwilling.
5. Reject the expectation for the child to adhere to adult-like social rules immediately.
6. Steer clear of screaming, yelling, or losing temper as a means of threatening the child into control. If necessary, leave the tantrum space after ensuring the child faces no physical harm.

Adhering to these guidelines fosters a more constructive approach to handling tantrums.

Tantrums in Teenagers

Certainly, the neocortical theory sheds light on the dynamics of tantrums, but what about teenagers? Despite possessing a developed prefrontal cortex (PFC), they often exhibit intense tantrums, which can prove extremely challenging to manage. Unlike toddlers who seek comfort after an outburst, teenagers may remain remorseless even after delivering hurtful comments. This concern prompts a frequent question in temper tantrum workshops: How can one control a teenager's tantrum and anger?

Once again, delving into the workings of brain function offers insights. Dr Merve Cikili Uytun, in her 2018 book, *Development Period of Prefrontal Cortex*, notes that the PFC nears complete development around 12-13 years but continues maturing into the twenties. While teenagers do not possess a fully mature PFC, their tantrums stem not from their immaturity. Recall that the reptilian brain activates in response to perceived threats, and for many teenagers, parents symbolise these threats—threats to their independence, social life, choice of friends, and creativity.

Effectively managing a teenager's tantrum involves demonstrating that you are not their adversary but a supporter of their endeavours. This doesn't entail abandoning values or discipline but rather rebuilding trust. Research by Langton and Berger in 2011 emphasises the correlation between family structure and adolescent health, highlighting the importance of open communication in fostering overall well-being. Thus, it becomes important for parents to engage in open conversations with their teenager, express understanding about the complexities of their lives, work on their adaptability, and make an effort to view the world from a millennial perspective. You can collaboratively establish basic rules on night-outs, studying, friends, screen time, and more. Find common ground. Periodically, offer plenty of hugs—a gesture that releases oxytocin, fostering a sense of belonging and bonding. While getting a hug from a teenager may be challenging, gentle touches like a pat on the back, a soft rub on the cheek, a gentle head pat, or even the trendier option of taking a selfie with a pout can serve as effective alternatives.

Effective Strategies for Parents

As discussed, temper tantrums consist of a sudden takeover by your child's primitive subconscious mind, which blocks inputs from the mature, thinking prefrontal cortex. The key to controlling tantrums lies in teaching your child how to manage emotions effectively.

Emotional intelligence is often overlooked but crucial in parenting. While delving into the extensive topic of emotional intelligence would require more than a few pages, here are some essential pointers:

1. **Unplanned Tantrums**

   Recognise that your child's tantrums aren't deliberate attempts to disrespect or embarrass you. Often, tantrums occur because they struggle to communicate their emotions effectively. By understanding this, you can respond with empathy and help them learn healthier ways to express themselves.

2. **H. I. T. Checklist**

   Address the basics—Hunger, Illness, and Tiredness. Many tantrums result from the child's brain not functioning optimally due to these factors. Ensuring your child isn't hungry, unwell, or exhausted can significantly reduce tantrums.

3. **Prepare and Plan**

   Children thrive on predictability. Minimise uncertainty by planning activities in advance. Inform your child about the expectations, such as behaviour in a mall or the limited choices for treats. Clear communication beforehand can mitigate tantrums, even if some resistance persists.

4. **Emotions Beyond Control**

   Tantrums manifest when the capacity for mature self-dialogue about emotions diminishes. The overwhelming surge of emotions hinders rational processing and prompts the non-thinking part of the brain to dictate the body's response. In essence, tantrums signify the emotional brain taking over from the thinking brain.

5. **Tantrums as Conversation**

   View tantrums as a form of communication. They signal that your child is grappling with emotional turmoil. Instead of seeing tantrums negatively, interpret them as your child's way of saying, 'Everything is falling apart.' Treat them with the same empathy and reassurance you would offer if your child expressed their distress verbally.

6. **Understanding and Handling Emotions**

   Teaching your child about emotions and their management is crucial. While comprehensive workshops delve deeply into this topic, a starting point involves explaining emotions to your child. Show them alternative, constructive ways to express and cope with their feelings. If you need more guidance, consider attending workshops or seeking one-on-one sessions for in-depth insights.

7. **Set Clear Limits**

   Establish early on the non-negotiable limits within your household. Physical abuse, such as hitting, slapping, or biting, should never be tolerated. Public humiliation is a steadfast rule—avoid any form of ridicule or embarrassment, as it can be more detrimental than physical discipline. A cardinal rule in parenting toddlers is to refrain from humiliating or ridiculing your child in public.

8. **Avoid Labeling Emotions**

   Emotions serve as your child's communication language. Since they may not have mastered verbal language completely, emotions are their natural way of expressing themselves. Discourage labelling emotions as 'bad' as it's similar to telling your child to stop communicating with you. Your reaction to their emotions determines whether you are perceived on the positive or negative side of the emotional spectrum.

9. **Lead by Example during Tantrums**

   Acknowledge that parents, like everyone else, have their share of challenging days. While there might be an inclination to shield your child from witnessing your occasional meltdown, consider using such moments as opportunities to showcase recovery. Demonstrate resilience, responsibility, and the ability to bounce back gracefully. Let your child see you as a resilient, responsible individual who acknowledges and rectifies mistakes.

Practical Tips for Managing Temper Tantrums

1. **Supportive Presence**

   As explained in the introduction regarding tantrum behaviour, the optimal approach is to allow the tantrum to run its course. During these challenging moments, it is essential to stay close to the child, maintaining a sense of calmness. If you can manage your emotions effectively, sit beside the child, providing the necessary emotional support without giving in to the tantrum. Simply offer your presence—serene, composed, yet unwavering in response to the tantrum.

2. **Comforting Embrace**

   A comforting embrace during a tantrum can work wonders in soothing your child's heightened emotions. Physical touch releases oxytocin, the 'feel-good' hormone, which helps reduce stress and anxiety. Holding your child close offers them a sense of security and reassurance, letting them know they are not alone in their feelings. This supportive gesture communicates empathy and understanding, fostering a deeper emotional connection between you and your child. Additionally, the calming effect of a hug can help regulate their emotions and facilitate quicker resolution of the tantrum.

3. **Firm Communication**

   Firm communication during a tantrum involves setting clear boundaries and expectations while maintaining a calm demeanour. By calmly but assertively stating limits and consequences, you establish a sense of structure and security for your child. This approach helps them understand that their behaviour is unacceptable while reinforcing their role as a consistent authority figure. Using simple and direct language, such as 'I understand you are upset, but yelling is not acceptable,' helps your child learn to express emotions constructively. Firm communication also teaches them valuable lessons about self-regulation and respect for others' boundaries.

4. **Timeout for Self-Reflection**

   Time-out for self-reflection offers children a chance to pause and regain control over their emotions. By removing them from the situation causing distress, they have space to calm down and reflect on their behaviour. During this time, encourage them to think about why they are upset and how they can express themselves more appropriately. It provides an opportunity for introspection and helps them develop emotional regulation skills. Once the time-out period is over, discuss their feelings and offer guidance on better ways to handle similar situations in the future.

5. **Reflective Recollection**

   Reflective reflection involves discussing the tantrum incident with your child after they have calmed down. It allows them to understand their emotions and behaviour and fosters self-awareness. Encourage them to express what triggered their tantrum and explore alternative ways to handle similar situations in the future. This process helps build emotional intelligence and problem-solving skills, empowering them to manage their emotions more effectively over time.

6. **Polite Persistence**

   Polite persistence involves calmly and consistently enforcing boundaries and expectations during a tantrum. By maintaining a composed demeanour and gently but firmly reinforcing rules, parents can help children understand appropriate behaviour. This approach emphasises patience and consistency, showing children that tantrums will not result in them getting their way. Over time, children learn to regulate their emotions and recognise the importance of respectful communication and self-control.

7. **Balanced Use of 'No'**

   The balanced use of 'no' involves judiciously setting limits while also offering alternatives or explanations to redirect tantrum behaviour. Instead of simply denying requests, parents can explain why certain actions or behaviours are not acceptable, providing a clear rationale for their decision. By offering choices or compromises when appropriate, parents empower children to feel heard and respected, reducing the likelihood of antrums. This approach promotes a sense of autonomy while still maintaining necessary boundaries and leads to better communication and cooperation between parent and child.

8. **Tantrum Buffer Planning**

   Tantrum buffer planning involves anticipating triggers and preparing strategies to defuse potential outbursts before they escalate. By identifying common triggers such as hunger, fatigue, or frustration, parents can pre-empt tantrums by addressing these underlying issues proactively. This may involve scheduling regular snack times, ensuring adequate rest, or offering calming activities to help regulate emotions. Additionally, having a toolkit of distraction techniques or calming strategies on hand can redirect attention and diffuse tension during tantrum-prone situations. By implementing proactive measures, parents can effectively mitigate tantrums and promote smoother interactions with their children.

9. **Protecting Self-Esteem**

   Protecting self-esteem during temper tantrums involves avoiding harsh criticism or negative labels that may damage a child's confidence and self-worth. Instead, focus on addressing the behaviour while affirming the child's inherent value and worth. By using positive reinforcement and praising efforts to calm down or communicate needs effectively, parents can help bolster their child's self-esteem and emotional resilience. Additionally, providing opportunities for the child to express their emotions and opinions in a safe and supportive environment can empower them to manage their feelings constructively, reducing the likelihood of tantrums in the future.

10. Role-Playing Life Lessons

Role-playing life lessons with your child can be a powerful tool in managing temper tantrums. By engaging in pretend scenarios, you can teach your child how to navigate challenging situations and express their emotions in a more constructive manner. Through role-play, children can practice problem-solving, empathy, and effective communication skills, which are essential for managing their emotions and behaviours. This interactive approach allows children to learn and internalise valuable lessons in a fun and engaging way, empowering them to handle tantrums more effectively in real-life situations.

11. Sharing Personal Stories

Sharing personal stories with your child can be a valuable strategy for managing temper tantrums. By recounting your own experiences, you can help your child understand that everyone faces challenges and struggles with emotions at times. Sharing how you coped with difficult situations can provide your child with practical strategies and reassurance that they are not alone in their feelings. Additionally, personal stories can strengthen your bond with your child and foster open communication, creating a supportive environment where they feel comfortable expressing themselves and seeking guidance when needed.

12. Developing Emotional Communication

Developing emotional communication skills with your child can be a powerful tool for managing temper tantrums. By teaching your child to identify and express their emotions effectively, you empower them to communicate their needs and frustrations in a constructive manner. Encouraging open dialogue about feelings and providing a safe space for expression can help your child feel understood and supported, reducing the likelihood of tantrums. Additionally, practising active listening and validating your child's emotions can strengthen your bond and promote a sense of trust and security as well as foster healthier emotional regulation in the long run.

13. Implementing Routine to Prevent Tantrums

Implementing a consistent routine can significantly reduce the occurrence of temper tantrums in children. Predictable schedules help children feel secure and in control, minimising anxiety and frustration that often lead to outbursts. By establishing regular mealtimes, nap schedules, and bedtime routines, you provide structure and stability, promoting emotional regulation and reducing the likelihood of meltdowns. Consistency also allows children to anticipate transitions and changes, empowering them to adapt more easily and cope with challenging situations. Additionally, incorporating calming activities into your routine, such as mindfulness exercises or quiet time before bed, can further support emotional well-being and temper tantrum prevention.

14. Utilising 'Feel' Words for Connection

Utilising 'feel' words for connection during temper tantrums can foster emotional understanding and empathy in children. By encouraging them to articulate their emotions, you validate their feelings and help them develop self-awareness and communication skills. Using phrases like 'I see you are feeling frustrated' or 'It looks like you are upset' demonstrates empathy and teaches children to recognise and express their emotions constructively. This approach promotes a sense of connection and trust between you and your child, reducing the intensity and duration of tantrums as they feel understood and supported in managing their feelings.

Chapter 3

FUSSY EATING

'My child eats every dish without a fuss,' said no Indian mom ever! If your child's picky eating has become a major parenting challenge, rest assured you are not alone. A study published in the *Journal of Nutrition Education and Behaviour* in September 2018 highlighted that the concern of dealing with a picky eater ranks high among parenting stressors.

The paradox that many millennial parents face is the transformation of an initially 'good eater' infant into a remarkably fussy 2-year-old, sitting at the dinner table with lips sealed tighter than any superhero's grip. It is puzzling to recall that your 6-month-old once enjoyed experimenting with semi-solids and embraced the messiness of mealtime. Yet, at 2 years old, coaxing any morsel into them feels like an uphill task! During these moments, even the most progressive-thinking mothers may doubt their mothering capabilities, wondering what turned their good eater into this unfamiliar toddler. But before self-criticism takes over, it is crucial to recognise that this transformation has a profound evolutionary connection. All children go through a phase of temporary fussiness; some outgrow it quickly, while others navigate through it for an extended period. The key factor determining the trajectory is how you handle your child's picky eating—scientifically or ignorantly!

To grasp this concept, let's journey back to the Stone Age. In those times, humans were primarily foragers and obtained their sustenance through hunting animals or consuming fruits and plants. Researchers at Philadelphia's Monell Chemical Senses Centre propose that the wariness toward food might be linked to the prevalence of toxic wild berries and plants. When our ancestors tried new foods, there was a risk of poisoning. Evolution wired our brains to be cautious about experimenting with unfamiliar foods and to remain vigilant about what goes into our mouths. This evolutionary dilemma becomes particularly pronounced in the modern world when a child reaches around 2 years of age. At this stage, toddlers have just learned to walk and gained access to various items they can put into their mouths. They no longer rely solely on trusted adult sources for food and are free to explore by putting anything they find into their mouths—be it food or a small object like a marble. The general message from the brain to toddlers becomes one of caution about eating. Anthropologists term this phenomenon the 'omnivore dilemma.' Therefore, if you find yourself puzzled by your toddler's shifting attitude towards food, an ancient evolutionary trait sheds light on what's unfolding in your contemporary household.

Elizabeth Cashdan, an anthropologist at the University of Utah in Salt Lake City, delved into the concept of dietary conservatism in her published study titled 'Adaptiveness of food learning and food aversions in children.' Her findings align broadly with the omnivore's dilemma, revealing that food neophobia tends to emerge between a child's second and third birthdays, and intensifies by the age of four. The evolutionary connection to poisonous plants continues to influence this phenomenon even in modern times. In support of this, Cashdan consulted the Utah Poison Control Centre and discovered that the primary cause of poisonings among 6 to 18-month-old children was eating houseplants, despite the presence of potentially toxic cleaning products and medicines in homes. But if the omnivore's dilemma is a significant factor in early childhood, then it should be observable in other omnivorous and herbivorous species, not exclusive to humans.

Dr David Watt's article in the *American Journal of Primatology* reports that infant gorillas exhibit adventurous eating habits, but slightly older gorillas become more cautious about new foods. Similarly, a book on primate social behaviour featured a chapter by J. M. Whitehead titled 'Development of feeding selectivity in mantled howling monkey,' which discussed the feeding habits of mantled howling monkeys in neotropic primate society. In this society, hungry juveniles observe their mothers' leaf-nibbling behaviour and mimic it. The study also revealed that adult howler monkeys refrain from sampling new foods in the presence of infants, conducting gastronomic experiments only when alone to ensure that youngsters do not imitate potentially unsafe eating behaviours until the adult can confirm the food's safety.

These studies underscore that toddler picky eating is a deeply ingrained evolutionary behaviour. However, a valuable strategy to overcome it is to sit with your toddler and enjoy a variety of foods in their presence. This exposure helps their brain categorise the foods on their plate as 'safe,' potentially initiating a positive relationship with a diverse range of foods. Turning mealtimes into a family affair was a crucial aspect of our upbringing in the 20th century, which perhaps explains why our mothers faced less difficulty in getting us to eat compared to the challenges we encountered with our own children in promoting a simple, healthy, balanced diet.

Additionally, an influential factor in shaping eating habits occurs even before a baby is born, and it is influenced by the mother's diet during pregnancy. Research indicates that we develop a predisposition to enjoy the flavours of foods our mothers consumed while pregnant. These flavours are transmitted through amniotic fluids and later through breast milk. As a result, the baby becomes 'familiar' with these tastes and is more likely to readily accept and enjoy these foods.

Beyond the omnipresent omnivore dilemma in most toddlers, another prevalent dietary phenomenon is the stark contrast in eating habits between siblings raised by the same parents. This familial diversity in food preferences is evident in my own household. Even my two daughters exhibit strikingly different attitudes toward food. While one considers it a basic survival necessity, the other not only enjoys food but also expresses a keen interest in the recipes and spices used in various dishes. This observation resonates with many households, prompting the question: Is picky eating a genetic trait? Can some children be inherently predisposed to be good eaters, while others are not? Part of this pickiness can be linked to specific genes that influence taste. A 2017 research study by Cole et al revealed that variants of the TAS2R38 gene play a role in determining picky eating tendencies in toddlers. This gene is responsible for coding taste receptors, which are situated on specialised taste cells bundled within taste buds on the human tongue's surface. These receptors can detect five fundamental tastes: sweet, sour, bitter, salty, and savoury flavours. However, attributing everything to genes and evolution oversimplifies the strong and intricate connection between food and memory. Culture plays a substantial role in shaping our children's attitudes toward eating. This leads us to the profound influence of food habits ingrained in different cultures. Consider the example of French children. Karen Le Billon, an American mom, relocated to France with her toddlers and discovered the positive and healthy eating culture there. She documented her experiences and insights in a book titled *French Kids Eat Everything*.

Le Billon observed that almost all French kids delight in and appreciate food. While they enjoy desserts, they are mindful of moderation. The approach French parents take toward food significantly contributes to why French toddlers are not picky eaters. Firstly, snacking between meals is discouraged in France. Snack food advertisements on French TV feature a large white banner (similar to warnings on cigarette packages) straightforwardly stating: 'For your health, avoid snacking between meals.' Meal preparation and consumption are viewed as family activities, with fresh, home-cooked meals being a daily norm in households. Children are educated about the proper approach to food both at home and in school. Food is not associated with fear of allergies, choking, hazards, stress, or mere necessity. The French culture instils in children a healthy and positive relationship with food.

In her book *Parenting Without Borders,* Christine Gross-Loh reflects on how her exposure to diverse world cultures has influenced her perspective on parenting. In the segment about food, she particularly highlights the relaxed attitude of Japanese mothers as they don't micromanage their children's menus and calorie intake. Gross-Loh recounts an incident at a playdate where a Japanese mother was surprised to learn that her child had not tasted candies yet. They were easy-going about distributing candies to keep the kids happy. Despite this relaxed approach to snacks and candies, Japan boasts the lowest rate of obesity globally. Japanese culture emphasises that children should taste everything. In many Japanese schools, meals feature a variety of cuisines, including Indian, French, and others, allowing children to experience diverse flavours. Japanese parents introduce a wide range of foods to their infants, from fish and beans to soy, soup, vegetables, and even octopus. The Japanese belief in exposing children to diverse tastes during infancy contributes to a broader palate as they grow up.

While Indian culture still emphasises home-cooked fresh meals, there is valuable wisdom to be gained from examining the approaches of different cultures towards food. Let's explore how we can adopt positive attitudes from various cultures in our Indian households.

Effective Strategies for Parents

1. An Empty Plate Doesn't Mean a Satiated Child

It is common for parents to insist that their child finishes everything on their plate. However, a child will naturally consume what they feel is appropriate for their appetite. When a healthy attitude toward mealtime is nurtured, a child will eat according to their needs and requirements.

2. **Maintain a Casual Demeanor**

   Children are adept at picking up on desperation. If they perceive how much their mealtime means to their mom, they might use it as a tool for manipulation or asserting power. Demonstrating that eating is the child's responsibility, not the parent's, can significantly shift the dynamics in your favour. This approach fosters a healthy attitude towards food and helps minimise conflicts during mealtime.

3. **Patience Is Key**

   Implementing new approaches or following helpful tips won't show immediate results. Your child may eat less initially, especially if accustomed to coercion or screen time during meals. Trust the process, stay committed to your goals, and understand that positive changes will unfold gradually. It is advisable to educate other caregivers in the house about your plan and seek their cooperation for the child's overall well-being.

4. **Avoid Feeding Your Child Out of Fear that They Won't Grow**

   Every child has a natural growth trajectory influenced by genetics. Body types are inherent, and attempting to force-feed won't alter these predispositions. For instance, if your elder daughter has a petite frame, and your younger one shows signs of being tall and broad, their growth patterns are predetermined. It is crucial to recognise and respect each child's unique characteristics rather than succumbing to concerns about growth that may lead to unnecessary force-feeding.

5. **Growth Is Best Measured through Mental and Physical Activity**

The true indicators of your child's well-being extend beyond the confines of a height and weight chart. Instead, pay attention to their mental engagement and physical vitality. A happy and content conduct serves as a more reliable gauge of their overall health than mere statistics on a growth chart.

6. **Avoid Excessive Reliance on Height and Weight Charts**

Though height and weight charts are valuable tools for monitoring your child's development, it is crucial to understand that they are not a blueprint for pushing your child into a specific percentile range through force-feeding. Rapid shifts from one percentile to another are unlikely, and attempting to achieve this through excessive feeding can lead to unnecessary stress.

It is also important to select a height and weight chart that is relevant to your child's demographic. American charts may not accurately reflect the growth patterns of Indian kids, and vice versa. Once you have the appropriate chart, track your child's progress by marking their birth weight and the first-year milestones. The key is to ensure that your child remains within the same percentile range as at birth. For instance, if your daughter was born in the 25th percentile and maintains that position, you are on the right track. While she may appear smaller than her peers, being within her percentile range is what matters.

7. **It Is Not Your Duty to Ensure the Child Is Fed**

In India, the responsibility of feeding a child is often placed solely on the mother. However, it is vital to recognise that the primary person responsible for a well-fed child should be the child themselves. Encouraging a child to eat independently from an early age fosters a sense of responsibility towards their own meals. If your 7-month-old enjoys playing with food, allow them to do so. It is their way of exploring different textures and developing an early familiarity with food, which, in turn, lays the foundation for a positive relationship with meals later on.

8. **The Crucial 6 to 18 Months Window**

   Pregnancy, breastfeeding, and weaning are the perfect opportunities to introduce a variety of foods. In many cultures, including India, semi-solid foods are typically introduced around the age of 6 months. This period, spanning from 6 to 18 months, plays a pivotal role in the development of taste preferences. It is essential to allow your infant to explore a diverse range of flavours, one bite at a time. Pay attention to your own diet as well; pregnant and breastfeeding mothers should also sample various foods. Flavours are known to be transmitted to your child through breast milk and amniotic fluids.

9. **Aim for 20-30 Minutes of Mealtime**

   Many parents find themselves stretched for hours, trying to coax their children into eating. This prolonged effort often leads to parental burnout. To avoid exhaustion and foster a healthy relationship with food, it is crucial to keep mealtime within a 30-minute timeframe, regardless of the child's age. Once the 30-minute mark is surpassed, consider clearing the table. This gentle practice encourages the child to complete meals promptly, instilling a sense of time awareness during meals.

10. Promote Inclusive Eating Habits

Some parents find themselves preparing a variety of dishes, hoping the child will accept at least one. However, this approach contradicts the nonchalant attitude that should prevail at the dinner table with kids. It is essential to encourage your child to eat what everyone else is having and convey that food is a natural need, meant to be enjoyed and nourish the body. While not every child may relish bitter gourd, it is acceptable to prepare an alternative dish on those days, like a curry or extra potatoes. However, refrain from creating an elaborate spread of pasta, noodles, and French fries exclusively for the child while the rest of the family enjoys bitter gourd.

11. Limit Junk Food Intake

While occasional indulgence in a packet of chips or a burger is acceptable, it is important not to equate it with a well-fed stomach. Celebrating if a fussy eater consumes an entire burger should be avoided. While these treats can break the routine and introduce variety, they shouldn't become the norm.

12. Gradually Eliminate Screen Time During Meals

If your child has developed a habit of watching YouTube while eating, it might initially seem convenient for parents. However, it is essential to wean them off this habit. Begin by introducing one meal without screen time and gradually extend it to other meals. This process may take weeks or even months, but it is acceptable to progress at a slow pace as long as you are actively working towards the goal of screen-free feeding time.

Practical Tips to Tackle Fussy Eating

1. Initiate Food Education at an Early Age

When introducing semi-solids to your infant at six months, it is vital to establish a positive relationship with food. Engage with your six-month-old about food, allowing them to explore textures and sensations. Although playing with food may create a mess, it is a valuable way for your child's developing brain to learn about food. Use your body language and expressions to emphasize the importance and joy of eating. Demonstrate your enjoyment by tasting the same food your child is eating and expressing delight. Even if you believe your child doesn't understand language yet, verbalise your thoughts. They can discern your emotions from your facial expressions and gestures, comprehending more than you might realise.

2. Play the Food Taster Game

Play is universally enjoyable for all human brains, especially for growing kids. Transform mealtime into a fun experience. One proven dinner table game, especially suitable for kids starting their food journey, is the food taster game. Food taster games are an excellent method to introduce a variety of foods to your child. Create a table on an A4 sheet with the first column listing the names of five different food items (vegetables, milk, non-veg, or anything you would like the child to eat). Title the next columns as Taste, Texture, Smell, and Colour. Pretend that your child is a food taster visiting your restaurant. They have to provide a report on various foods. For instance, if the first item is mushrooms, the child takes a bite and writes whether the dish is sweet, sour, spicy, or bitter. Then they describe the texture, smell, and colour of the dish. This engaging game encourages your picky eater to at least try new foods.

3. Engage Your Child in Menu Planning before Meals

To avoid dinner table battles and ensure your child eats what's prepared, a great strategy is involving them in deciding the dinner menu. Mealtime fussiness often involves a power play, with the child asserting control over whether to open their mouth. When the child has a say in the menu, they are less likely to resist once the meal is cooked and served. Provide options for them to choose from in order to avoid a completely blank slate to prevent everyday choices like French fries or pasta.

For example, you can create a 'recipes for this week' list containing 10-12 dishes, predominantly healthy meals with 1 or 2 options for junk food. Once a dish is prepared, mark it off the list to prevent repetitive selections, especially of junk food. Ensure the list includes a mix of dishes your child enjoys and some you wish to introduce into their food journey, such as paneer or rajma-rice, along with a few vegetables like bottled gourd or radish. This approach empowers children by offering them choices while gradually introducing new foods. Plan your weekly recipe list in advance, perhaps on Saturday night, to ensure you have time to gather the necessary ingredients.

4. **Make Mealtimes Enjoyable**

If you have had a negative experience with a certain food, your brain may form a permanent link between that food and the negative outcome. Thus, it is crucial to create positive associations with food by associating mealtimes with positive and joyful memories. Approach dinner time with a sense of joy and curiosity. Use this opportunity to connect with your child and learn more about their day. I enjoy hearing about my kids' experiences at school or the park during meals, and I also share stories from my own life, such as my workday or a coffee outing with friends. If your child isn't very talkative about their day or is in the pre-teen stage of giving short answers, mealtime can serve as an icebreaker, especially if you are serving a favourite dish. Turn dinner into a chance to open up your teen's heart and mind, using something as simple as chicken curry as a gateway to conversation.

5. **Make Food Exciting**

Research shows that the first impression of taste is often visual. Foods that are visually appealing are perceived as more appetising. Present meals in creative arrangements, such as smiley faces or shapes, and allow your child to explore the textures of their food. In addition to visual appeal, colour and texture also influence food acceptance. A recent Tamil blockbuster featuring a chef with anosmia (loss of sense of taste) shows how the brain processes food and taste through all senses. Before tasting food and forming connections in the brain, it is crucial to stimulate other senses with visual and textural cues. Plate the food thoughtfully and encourage your child to interact with it, squashing and exploring its texture. This helps establish a healthy relationship with food for the future.

6. **Transform One Meal into a Family Affair**

   In our fast-paced lives, sitting down together for every meal can be challenging for the entire family. However, if possible then try to have at least one parent present during meals, especially in the early years. Children possess mirror neurons that imitate parental behaviour. If you enthusiastically enjoy all your veggies, there is a higher likelihood that your child will accept vegetables too. Ensure you share at least one meal with your kids at the dining table. Use this time to discuss your day, experiences, and feelings.

7. **Introduce Engaging Dinner Table Games**

   You can make your child look forward to mealtime by incorporating entertaining dinner table games. Not only are these games fun, but they also make meals more enjoyable for the child. Replace screen time with dinner games that offer the same adrenaline rush. From storytelling sessions where each family member adds a line to the story to trivia quizzes related to the day's events, there are numerous ways to engage your child and foster a positive mealtime atmosphere. These games not only encourage interaction but also create lasting memories and strengthen family bonds around the dinner table.

For a list of dinner table games, you can write to me at nirvanamaa@gmail.com.

8. **Encourage Table Etiquettes**

   Empower the child to choose utensils, grab a napkin, and set the dinner table for everyone. Involving children in household chores imparts crucial life lessons. A Harvard review revealed that individuals who shouldered household responsibilities as children often grew into successful leaders and CEOs. Food-related chores, such as table setting, dishwashing, and putting utensils away, are excellent ways to teach responsibility and enhance your child's relationship with food.

   During the Covid lockdown, many families implemented chore allocation as a way to bond and instil a sense of responsibility in their children. Bringing back that chore list you once introduced can reignite those positive habits. If you previously hesitated due to your child's age or the availability of household help, consider breaking that mental barrier. Allocating age-appropriate chores to your child, regardless of their age, can foster independence and teach valuable life skills from an early age.

9. **Large-Plate Brain Hack**

   Have you ever noticed how fancy restaurants or five-star hotels serve food on large plates with tiny portions? It is not just a quirk but a clever visual trick to encourage guests to eat more and order additional dishes, boosting profits for these establishments. When the brain sees a large plate with small portions, it perceives less food, tricking us into feeling like we have eaten less. Apply the same principle with your kids by serving their meals on larger plates. This way, they won't feel overwhelmed by the amount of food, as the plate appears relatively empty. It is a simple hack to encourage healthier eating habits without resistance. Give it a try today!

10. Ensure the Child Doesn't Fear the Food Bowl

Forcing children to eat can have detrimental effects on their relationship with food. It often results in lower food intake and may lead to a reliance on being fed by parents well into their older years. If your seven-year-old still expects to be fed, it could be because she was never given the opportunity to feed herself due to concerns about inadequate intake. While force-feeding or allowing children to eat while distracted by screens may temporarily increase food intake, it can lay the groundwork for an unhealthy relationship with food in the long run. The association between food and emotions is powerful. For example, if a child's brain links stress, fear, or indifference (such as mindlessly eating while watching screens) with food, it may contribute to lifelong struggles with food and health. Therefore, it is crucial to avoid establishing this negative connection from an early age.

Chapter 4

Academic Pressure

Indians are known for their high IQs, a combination of innate intelligence and the cultural emphasis on academic excellence instilled by parents. This multi-level influence has propelled Indians to the forefront of various academic fields globally, often contributing to groundbreaking achievements in institutions like NASA and Harvard. However, alongside these triumphs, alarming headlines have emerged. According to the National Crime Bureau Records, an unsettling reality unfolded in 2018, with 24 students taking their lives daily, translating to one student every hour succumbing to academic pressures or failures. A 2015 survey by Born Smart, a parenting website, revealed that 62 per cent of parents admitted to resorting to corporal punishment, with homework, stress, and tradition identified as primary triggers. Additionally, the 2012 Lancet Report indicated that India holds the unfortunate distinction of having the highest suicide rate among youth aged 15 to 29 worldwide. Also, in 2017, a *Hindustan Times* report further emphasised the link between academic pressure, exam failures, and the rise in frustration and helplessness among students, often leading to tragic outcomes. Kota has gained notoriety in recent years, thanks to web series like *Kota Factory* and numerous reports highlighting the intense pressure students face there, particularly concerning engineering entrance exams. Tragically, some students have even taken their own lives as a result of this pressure.

The alarming statistic of one child taking their own life every hour is a distressing plea for immediate attention, placing unprecedented academic pressure as one of the top concerns for millennial parents. The conflicting thoughts on how to address this issue create a cacophony in our minds: Should we disregard the importance of schools and exams, and should we stop caring about which college our children attend? The answer to this question lies in seeking practical and scientific answers becomes imperative.

Firstly, redefining academic excellence is essential. While many equate it solely with good grades, this correlation is scientifically flawed. Excelling in tests often reflects strong memory skills rather than true intelligence. In later years of life, particularly during alumni gatherings, it is a common topic of discussion that the individual who excelled academically in class isn't always the one who achieves the most success later in life. This leads us to ponder: What truly constitutes intelligence?

Understanding intelligence proves challenging, given the limited knowledge about the intricacies of the human brain. Despite the prevalence of brain apps and purported genius-boosting products in the market, they often exploit parental aspirations rather than relying on sound scientific principles. The complexity of intelligence extends beyond current understanding, urging a more nuanced approach to nurturing our children's potential.

Albert Einstein once remarked, 'Creativity is Intelligence having fun,' which provides a valuable perspective on intelligence from one of the most brilliant minds in history. Dean Burnett, in his renowned book *The Idiot Brain,* delves into the intricate nature of human intelligence and cites various studies that highlight its multifaceted origins. Unlike a pinpointed area in the brain, intelligence comprises diverse modalities such as memory, creativity, verbal fluency, mathematical ability, reasoning, and more; simply put, a collaborative effort of the entire brain.

The evolution and complexity of human intelligence set us apart as a species. Our diverse forms of intelligence, displayed by individuals ranging from ace cricketers to doctors, demonstrate its versatility beyond academic realms. As the most intelligent species on earth, our journey from discovering fire to space travel in a few centuries shows the remarkable capabilities of our intelligence.

Despite our inherent intelligence, the question arises: Can we enhance it? Can parents boost the IQ of their children? Educational toys, an evergreen favourite among young parents, have long been employed to stimulate toddler IQ. While activities like puzzles, memory games, crosswords, and sudoku contribute to mental activity, they predominantly target specific aspects of intelligence, such as memory or mathematical abilities. What we need to understand is that the brain functions like a muscle, and the part you exercise more tends to enhance. This principle is underscored by a notable 2000 *Nature* paper on London taxi drivers, whose brain scans revealed a larger hippocampus, associated with navigation, compared to others. The research suggests that prolonged navigating experience led to structural changes in the hippocampus.

Therefore, the key to fostering intelligence in children is not a single milk powder or game but exposing their brains to diverse stimuli. Unlike an overnight process, it requires time. Restricting children to solely 'educational toys' can lead to burnout and an aversion to academics. A mix of toys, life experiences, creativity, freedom, love, and praise is crucial.

Surprisingly, love and praise play a role in enhancing intelligence. A 1968 study, 'Pygmalion in the Classroom,' revealed that when teachers were falsely informed that certain students were gifted, those students, though average test-takers, performed better due to the encouragement from their teachers. Therefore, fostering a love for knowledge, praising learning efforts, and avoiding belittlement for struggling with academic concepts can alleviate academic pressure for both parents and children.

Effective Strategies for Parents

1. Cultivate the Joy of Learning

Encouraging the innate curiosity of young minds is a powerful strategy for their early development. By tapping into the natural learning mode, you can harness the unparalleled neuron development that occurs in the first two years. Establishing a daily learning routine creates a structured yet flexible environment for exploration and discovery. This not only enhances cognitive development but also lays a strong foundation for a lifelong love of learning. As young brains are exceptionally receptive during this period, incorporating diverse activities and stimuli into their routine fosters a well-rounded and adaptable mindset.

2. **Delegate Academic Responsibility Appropriately**

   It is essential to understand that your child is ultimately accountable for their grades. While it is valuable to familiarise yourself with the subjects, promoting independent study is key to academic growth and nurturing a sense of personal responsibility. Encouraging your child to take ownership of their learning journey instils valuable skills such as time management and self-discipline. By striking a balance between support and personal responsibility, you empower your child to develop a proactive approach to their education and foster a genuine interest in the subjects they study.

3. **Separate Learning from Grades**

   Recognise the heightened stress associated with exams and grades, and take proactive steps to shield your children from unnecessary pressure. Rather than solely focusing on grades, prioritise fostering a clear understanding of concepts. Encourage a growth mindset that views challenges as opportunities for learning and improvement and shifts the focus from performance metrics to the acquisition of knowledge. By creating a supportive environment that values the learning process over grades, you promote a healthier perspective on academic achievement and equip your children with coping mechanisms to navigate stress in a constructive manner.

4. **Shift the Focus from Memory**

   Engaging in memory games is a fantastic way to boost your child's memory skills. However, it is crucial to realise that grades don't always equate to profound learning. In our educational system, they often primarily reflect good memory rather than genuine comprehension. While memory games contribute to cognitive abilities, true understanding involves a deeper grasp of concepts. Encourage your child to go beyond rote memorisation and focus on understanding the underlying principles of the subjects they study. By emphasising comprehension over memorisation, you guide them toward a more holistic and enduring approach to learning that goes beyond the constraints of standardised assessments.

5. **Infuse Joy into Learning**

   Rediscovering the inherent fun in learning, which children naturally embrace, is a transformative approach. Counteract the impact of years of performance-focused education by making academic concepts enjoyable for your child. Incorporate interactive and playful methods into their study routine to make the educational journey engaging and exciting. This approach not only nurtures a positive attitude towards education but also promotes a lifelong love for acquiring knowledge.

6. **Broaden Perspective on Learning**

   Expanding the scope of learning is crucial beyond the confines of homework and test preparation. Instead of limiting knowledge to the syllabus, encourage your child to explore related topics, fostering a more profound understanding of the subject matter. By broadening their view of learning, you promote a mindset that values curiosity and independent inquiry. By instilling the habit of exploring beyond the prescribed curriculum, you empower your child to embrace a lifelong journey of intellectual curiosity and discovery.

7. **Embrace Creativity**

   Embracing creativity is a cornerstone of holistic education. Thus, it becomes important to encourage children to explore their creative instincts and foster a range of essential skills. Creative expression enhances problem-solving abilities, promotes critical thinking, and nurtures effective communication. By incorporating arts, music, and other creative outlets into their learning journey, children develop a well-rounded skill set that extends beyond the boundaries of traditional subjects. So, as educators and parents, fostering an environment that values and nurtures creativity empowers children to think outside the box and fosters a lifelong appreciation for imaginative exploration and self-expression.

8. **Prioritise Play**

   Harnessing the scientifically proven benefits of play and exercise can significantly improve focus and concentration in children. Recognising the potential shortfall of physical activity in millennial children, it is essential to address this aspect to release pent-up energy and enhance their ability to concentrate during study sessions. Incorporating regular breaks for physical activities, such as outdoor play or structured exercises, not only promotes overall well-being but also contributes to increased cognitive function. Scientifically, physical movement has been linked to improved attention spans and enhanced memory retention. By integrating play and exercise into your child's routine, you provide a holistic approach to their development, ensuring that both their physical and cognitive needs are met for optimal learning outcomes.

Practical Tips to Mitigate Academic Pressure

1. **Transform Lessons into Stories or Drama**

   Leveraging the potency of human visual and pictorial memory is a powerful strategy for enhancing learning experiences. Infusing educational content with elements of storytelling and drama can work wonders in capturing and retaining a child's attention. By incorporating narratives, visuals, and dramatic elements, you create a multisensory learning environment that caters to diverse learning styles. This approach makes the learning process more engaging and enhances the ability to remember and recall information.

   Engaging in language lessons can take on a theatrical approach, with both you and your child assuming the roles of different characters. For math and science concepts, hands-on experiments and experiences in nature often yield the best understanding. For instance, teaching counting is more effective in a park setting, where your child can count the red flowers around them. Tailoring subjects to your child's interests can further stimulate their curiosity and make learning more enjoyable.

2. **Infuse Humour into Study Time**

   A stressed brain doesn't absorb information effectively. Stress for a child might be as trivial as a broken pencil.

Humour signals the brain that the situation isn't as stressful as it seems and prevents the release of adrenaline.

Here's a conversation I had with my kids when they were younger, and I needed to teach them words with ambiguous spellings.

> Me: 'T was a teacher. G and H were her chatterbox students. T always told them to be silent. Now, whenever there's T, G and H stay silent. That's why "light" is spelt as L-I-G-H-T but pronounced as "Lite" because . . . ?'
>
> My Daughter (drawing fingers on the letters G and H): 'G and H have fingers on their lips with T around.'

Such conversations often resulted in plenty of laughter during our study sessions. It was a win-win situation, strengthening our mother-daughter bond while also benefiting my daughter's developing brain.

3. Embrace Nature Walks

Forest preschools, prominent in Nordic countries, teach through nature which contributes to the long-term academic success of children. This can be seen through the performance of Swedish adults in standardised tests. The training they receive in preschool years centres around nurturing a love for knowledge, nature, and curiosity—a foundation for academic and scientific excellence.

Nearly every concept, including intricate engineering principles, finds its counterpart in nature. After all, who better than nature itself to serve as the ultimate architect! Thus, relate all the subjects your child is studying to examples found in the natural world. The brain is inherently inclined to grasp and retain knowledge when it's rooted in nature-based learning.

4. **Encourage Independent Exploration**

In the journey of parenting, the goal is to gradually make your child less dependent on you. This principle extends to academics and would encourage children to seek answers independently and resist the impulse to finish homework quickly. For instance, if your child writes '8' as the answer for '4x3,' the instinct may be to interrupt. However, it is best to wait until the child completes the work independently before offering assistance and curtail the temptation to intervene when your child struggles with a part of their homework or worksheets.

5. **Stimulate Curiosity Beyond the Syllabus**

It is important to realise that learning institutes were established to inculcate curiosity, thinking and exploration. Early gurukuls did not have books or syllabi as the primary aim of having a dedicated centre for learning was to expose the young minds towards independent thinking and learn from gurus who have been pursuing knowledge and have garnered enough information about how nature works. That is why having a well-rounded approach towards topics in your child's academic syllabi is very important.

Stimulating curiosity beyond the syllabus is a key aspect of fostering a love for learning in children. Encouraging them to explore topics of interest outside the prescribed curriculum not only enhances their overall knowledge but also cultivates a sense of intellectual curiosity. By exposing children to a diverse range of subjects and encouraging them to ask questions, we fuel their innate desire to understand the world around them.

For example, when teaching your child about planets, share the story of Copernicus, who demonstrated that all planets orbit the sun and that the earth is not the centre of the solar system. This narrative not only captivates with its intrigue but also integrates an isolated concept into the broader story of space exploration, such as today's missions to Mars.

6. Craft a Song for Challenging Concepts

Music has a unique impact on memory, often creating 'earworms' that linger in our minds. Transforming academic concepts into catchy tunes facilitates easier memorisation. When my 6-year-old struggled with the concept of time, we composed a playful song that not only clarified the chronological order of terms but also delved into the scientific meaning of a 'year.' This two-line song became her mnemonic key, effortlessly guiding her through the subject.

'Second, minutes, hours, day, week, month Year means the earth has gone around the sun!'

7. Establish a Timetable for Academic Activities

It is important for kids to be disciplined and up to date with what's being taught in school. Dedicate specific times for syllabus-related tasks and encourage exploration during other periods of the day. Ensure that all caregivers are aware of the child's timetable. Providing children with a structured daily routine alleviates insecurities and imparts early lessons in discipline and delayed gratification.

I recall advising my child to allocate 3-4 p.m. daily to review school material, with the added task of sharing a fun fact beyond the curriculum each day. Searching for these fun facts exposed her to numerous relevant and exciting stories about topics from her curriculum.

8. **Promote Diverse Role Models**

While society often glorifies celebrity role models, expose your child to a broader spectrum. Discuss scientists, astronauts, and teachers as sources of inspiration. Avoid limiting choices to class toppers—many academic role models boast fascinating stories and diverse backgrounds.

Visiting the Secmol School of Learning in Leh, founded by Mr Sonam Wangchuk, was a cherished item on my bucket list for years. He has long been an inspiration to me, so finally experiencing the school firsthand felt like a pilgrimage. Sharing my excitement and stories about meeting my hero with my daughters encouraged them to seek inspiration from individuals excelling in academics, sports, social work, and beyond, rather than solely relying on glamour and media.

9. **Embrace Unusual Storytelling**

Encourage your child to share imaginative, even bizarre, stories. Confining a child's thinking is a disservice to humanity. Creativity, often overlooked, is a crucial aspect of intelligence—extending beyond arts and crafts to limitless imagination in thought, understanding, and practice.

Imagine a world devoid of the boundless creativity found in stories like *Alice in Wonderland* and *Fantastic Beasts*. These imaginative tales serve as fuel for our minds, igniting curiosity and sparking innovation. Without such imaginative narratives, our intellectual landscape would be considerably less rich and vibrant.

10. Engage in the 'LIE Game'

Challenge your child to creatively reinterpret everything around them for half an hour. Whether calling a blue bottle a pink oxygen tank, the key is imaginative logic. Refrain from laughing, regardless of how wild the answer is. In this game, playing outside the rules knows no bounds. Engaging in such activities not only fosters enjoyment but also strengthens the bond between you and your child, creating countless moments of joy and connection.

11. Understand Your Child's Strengths and Weaknesses

While our children share our physical traits, they aren't simply extensions of our lives. Their strengths may differ, and their life's path isn't about filling gaps in our own. Encourage your children to explore their own unique strengths and talents, guiding them to embrace their individuality rather than conforming to expectations. By nurturing their interests and passions, they can carve out their own paths in life, independent of our desires. Remember, their journey is theirs alone, and supporting them in discovering and developing their potential is one of the greatest gifts we can give as parents.

12. **Share Stories About Your Childhood and Academics**

    Instead of fabricating stories—for example, that you were a high-achieving student, especially when you were not—to push academic performance, be genuine about your own school experiences. When parents humanise themselves and avoid acting like infallible gods, meaningful dialogues with kids become possible. They won't see you as an intimidating figure but as a relatable guide. This honesty also builds trust and strengthens the parent-child bond, creating a supportive environment for academic growth and personal development.

13. **Address Fears Positively**

    Keep an eye out for developing fears in specific subjects and address them positively. Expecting instant excellence isn't realistic. Stress can hinder learning, activating the brain's 'flight-fight-fight' response, leading to anxiety and a survival mindset. Avoid making a big deal about studies; otherwise, the brain perceives them as a threat. Identify any academic-related fears in your child and address them promptly. By not fixating on fear and instead directing your attention toward finding ways to overcome it, you can help your child build confidence and resilience in facing academic challenges.

14. **Embrace Continuous Learning**

    Demonstrate that learning extends beyond grades—it's about personal development. Children follow what they see. If they witness you exploring new territories, they are more likely to embark on similar paths with confidence. Thus, by modelling a mindset of curiosity and embracing new challenges, you illustrate to your children that learning is a lifelong journey filled with opportunities for self-discovery and improvement.

I thoroughly enjoy my 'Sunday learning' sessions. Last year, I delved into learning Spanish through an audiobook, and in 2020, I completed a course on Cognitive Neuroscience on Udemy. Demonstrating a commitment to lifelong learning not only sets a positive example for children but also helps keep the mind sharp and youthful.

Chapter 5

Body Image

Is it fair for a young girl to go into depression or even worse, take her own life because of dissatisfaction with her body? As parents, we certainly hope not! But this harsh reality confronts us, especially as millennial parents. We have all experienced the pressures of our teenage years—craving the ideal body, seeking attention from a crush, and wanting to be part of the popular crowd. Moments of self-doubt about our appearance are a natural part of adolescence, and it is driven by new hormones and thoughts. However, why has this issue become more severe in the current millennium?

The intensity of this problem is exacerbated by the omnipresence of social media and the constant intrusion of trolls into every aspect of our kids' lives who pass judgement on their looks. It cannot be stressed enough why fostering a healthy and positive body image in our children should be a top priority for every millennial parent.

The millennial era has introduced several new terms, one of them being 'body shaming.' But what does it entail? Body shaming involves ridiculing individuals based on their physical appearance, be it body shape or skin colour. These attributes are not choices; they are inherent aspects—like being born with a specific skin colour due to ancestral heritage or having a slower metabolic rate leading to weight gain. Body shaming unfolds with dual facets. Initially, one might assume it emerges from bullies taunting individuals based on their body types. Addressing this aspect aligns with conventional approaches to handling bullies, as further discussed in Chapter 8. However, an additional layer to body shaming exists—many children harbour self-loathing sentiments about their bodies without any external bullying. This deeper issue roots itself in traditions, cultural ideals, and the influence of social media. Matrimonial ads frequently express preferences for 'fair-skinned girls,' while society upholds the norm that 'thin is beautiful.' Additionally, with social media's rise, celebrities enter every household, which leads aspiring young individuals to believe their favourite actors or actresses effortlessly attain the perfection portrayed on Instagram.

The important point to note here is that whether a child feels body shamed due to bullies, peer pressure, unrealistic beauty standards, social media influence, or self-criticism, the toll on a developing mind can be profoundly damaging. Consequences of this can extend from anxiety and depression to severe eating disorders like bulimia and anorexia, with some cases even culminating in suicide.

Despite common perceptions, many parents still hold the misconception that body shaming and its associated issues predominantly afflict Western societies. Dr Udipi Gauthamadas, a Chennai-based neuro-behavioural medicine expert specialising in treating eating disorders, highlights that disturbed eating attitudes and behaviours affect about 25 to forty per cent of adolescent girls and around twenty per cent of adolescent boys.

In 2015, France took a commendable and bold step by enacting a law stipulating that any photograph subjected to Photoshop alterations must include a disclaimer about the edits made. Whether adjusting waistlines, lightening skin tones, or airbrushing features for perceived improvements, the images must disclose these modifications. Following suit, Getty, a major online photo stock platform, implemented a ban on photoshopped images of models starting in 2017. This initiative was warmly received by body-positive activists worldwide, as it serves as an effective means to shield growing kids from distorted versions of reality.

However, a perplexing question arises: Why do countless individuals in our society remain untouched by such measures and continue to harbour ingrained notions of body shape and colour discrimination? This prompts an investigation into whether the persistent favouritism for fair skin and slim bodies has an evolutionary basis. Is our inclination toward a specific physical appearance hardwired within us?

A morally challenging study conducted in the U.K. by Dr Slater and his team provides some insights. Their research revealed that humans are born with a predisposition for attractive faces. Alan Slater and colleagues at the University of Exeter presented paired images of faces to babies as young as one day old and noted that infants spent more time fixated on the more attractive face. Slater asserts, 'Attractiveness is not in the eye of the beholder; it's innate to a newborn infant.'

The innate preference for attractive faces in newborns, evident from as early as one day old, suggests a hardwired idea of beauty ingrained in the human brain through evolution. This predisposition raises the question:

What is this hardwired standard of beauty that even an infant recognises?

Research points to 'symmetry' as a crucial factor. According to Anthony Little, a psychologist at the University of Stirling in Scotland, subtle differences in symmetry characterise people's faces, with each face exhibiting a unique form of asymmetry. Despite these differences, many faces appear symmetrical to us, creating a perception of normalcy and garnering our preference.

Additionally, the factor of race plays a role. In gaze tests conducted with infants a few months old (not newborns), it was observed that older infants, having gained experience with people and society, gaze longer at the faces of individuals from their own race. Studies conducted at the University of Delaware revealed that babies' brains are more adept at processing faces from their own racial group, leading infants to quickly develop a preference for faces of their own race.

While science indicates a preference for attractive faces and faces of our own race, it is crucial not to use these findings to justify or dismiss the harmful effects of body shaming. The purpose of highlighting these insights is not to condone beauty prejudice as an inevitable outcome of brain wiring but to emphasise that addressing this social issue requires proactive measures. Wishing it away, protesting, or ignoring it won't suffice. Positive conditioning from an early age, facilitated through parenting, emerges as the key to combating this societal problem.

Educating children about positive body image, equipping them to handle bullying, and fostering empathetic discussions about body and skin colour are essential steps. A fundamental principle is to refrain from making comments about a child's weight, even with constructive intentions. Emphasising a child's weight can reinforce the idea that thinness is a paramount ideal, a message already prevalent in various aspects of their lives. This pressure can lead to self-consciousness, lower self-esteem, and an increased risk of depression, affecting kids of all body types.

Encouraging fitness in your household is important, considering the sedentary lifestyle, poor eating habits, and increasing stress levels. Obesity poses a significant threat to the future generation's health, making discussions around fitness essential. However, these conversations should focus on overall well-being rather than weight or achieving specific body frames.

Jennifer Harriger, a developmental psychologist, advises against singling out children or pointing fingers. Instead, promote family goals that foster healthy behaviours. For instance, suggest activities like going for walks or hiking together as a family. When addressing dietary habits, aim for diverse and colourful food choices collectively. Also, avoid categorising foods as 'good' or 'bad,' as moralising food reinforces harmful associations.

If your child experiences fat-shaming from peers, don't dismiss their feelings. Simple reassurances like 'it doesn't matter' may not be effective, as your child does care about others' opinions. Acknowledge the hurtful words and empathise with your child. Use the opportunity to discuss broader societal issues and inform that our culture places undue emphasis on looks. Reinforce the idea that differences make individuals special, fostering a sense of self-worth and appreciation for diversity.

Effective Strategies for Parents

1. **Stay Informed and Aware**

   While it is essential not to overwhelm ourselves with the stress of potential dangers, living in a bubble isn't the solution either. Stay vigilant and attentive to any warning signs or signals your child may be displaying. If you see a sudden change in behaviour or personality in your child, be prompt in opening a dialogue with your child about it. Early detection of issues such as sexual abuse, molestation, low self-esteem, and depression can significantly reduce the likelihood of these problems escalating.

2. **Address Body Image Challenges Early**

   Social issues affecting children often manifest long before adolescence. And though it might seem unimaginable for a 5-year-old to experience a blow to their self-esteem from being called 'fat,' it's crucial to acknowledge that societal norms and pressures have evolved. As parents, we must adapt our parenting approaches and priorities to address these changing dynamics effectively. Reports of minors experiencing trauma or engaging in self-harm emphasise the importance of addressing these concerns proactively. Early intervention can make a significant difference in preventing long-term consequences.

3. **Amplified Impact of Social Media**

   Unlike the days when we could disconnect for a while, today's kids are constantly bombarded by social media. The influence of social platforms exacerbates issues like body image, as they are consistently exposed to curated images of seemingly flawless lives. Helping children navigate these pressures becomes essential, considering the overwhelming noise generated by social media. Avoiding exposure to social media until at least the age of 15 can serve as a beneficial guideline.

As one of the few content creators abstaining from social media, I made this deliberate choice to demonstrate to my children that exceptional work can still pave the way for a successful career through word-of-mouth and genuine human connections, such as my workshops. Initially, there was a decline in my reach after stepping away from social media, but by implementing some strategic changes and focusing on public relations efforts, I was able to regain the attention of a significant portion of my audience without relying on social media platforms.

4. **Focus on Fitness, Not Weight**

   Avoid discussing your weight issues or expressing dissatisfaction with your body in front of your child. Emphasise the importance of fitness and well-being instead. Be mindful of the words you use and frame your goals in a positive light. For example, talk about wanting to be fitter, improving stamina, or lifting more weights. This helps cultivate a positive attitude towards health.

5. **Emphasise Body Functionality**

   Encourage your child to understand and appreciate their body from the inside out, focusing on its capabilities rather than its appearance. Highlight the amazing things their body can do, such as performing cartwheels, playing musical instruments with their fingers, or excelling at sports. While it's normal for kids to have a desire to look nice, incorporate other values into your conversations to broaden their perspective. For instance, if your daughter is enchanted by princesses, inquire about her role or expertise as a princess, reinforcing that her value extends beyond her appearance.

6. **Avoid Weight-Based Gossip**

   Refrain from engaging in gossip sessions, especially in front of children, that focus on weight or body size. As a true friend, choose to encourage fitness rather than mock someone behind their back. Treat others as you would want to be treated yourself.

7. **Address Bullying Behaviour**

   If you discover that your child is using derogatory terms like 'fat' to describe someone, initiate a conversation to understand their perspective. Instead of harsh consequences, foster empathy by saying, 'People come in different shapes and sizes.' Encourage a calm, positive, and patient approach to instil lessons in empathy. Empathy is a gradual development in children, requiring consistent small efforts each day.

8. **Adopt a Fitness Regimen**

   Demonstrate a positive body image by incorporating your own fitness routine into daily life. Whether it's the gym, weight training, yoga, Zumba, or Pilates, let your child witness your commitment to health and fitness.

9. **Involve Your Child in Fitness Activities**

Despite the challenges of working out with a toddler, find ways to include them in your fitness routine. Consider hiring a home yoga trainer, allowing your child to participate by imitating your movements, crawling under body bridges, or sitting in your lap during exercises like Padmasana (lotus pose).

10. **Choose Nutrient-Rich Meals**

While indulging in tasty treats like burgers or pizzas is enjoyable, emphasise the appeal of healthy alternatives. Demonstrate that grilled fish or perfectly cooked chicken breast can be as delicious as a cheeseburger. Transform traditional burgers into a healthier option by using wheat buns, baking the patty instead of frying, and opting for a vegetable patty instead of a potato one. Illustrate that food can be both nutritious and flavourful.

11. **Embrace Occasional Indulgences**

Despite focusing on exercise and sensible eating, teach your child the importance of occasional indulgences. Emphasise that enjoying cake, chocolate, or doughnuts is not a crime but should be done in moderation. Life is meant to be lived to the fullest, and treats are part of the experience.

12. **Understand Your Child's Friends and Their Values**

Recognise the significant influence peers have on a child's life. Understanding the dynamics of your child's social circle is crucial, as the company they keep plays a pivotal role in shaping their personality and perspectives. This knowledge can be instrumental in addressing various challenges your child might encounter in the future.

Practical Tips to Combat Unhealthy Body Image Issues

1. **Integrate Family Exercise into Daily Routine**

   Incorporate enjoyable physical activities like Bollywood dance, jump rope sessions, or mindful breathing exercises into your family's daily routine. Lead by example and emphasise the significance of allocating time for exercise. When children witness their parents prioritising health and fitness, they are likely to follow suit. So parents, it's time to dust off those running shoes or cycling shorts from hibernation and do yourself and your kids a great favour!

2. **Educate Them about Photoshop and Celebrity Imagery**

   Discuss the prevalent use of Photoshop in magazines and celebrity images. Highlight that many celebrities, even those portraying 'I woke up like this' moments, heavily rely on makeup and digital enhancements. You can easily find such content with a quick Google search. Moreover, by injecting some humour into this serious topic by sharing funny memes that expose Photoshop fails will ensure your child is aware of the realities behind seemingly perfect images.

3. **Prioritise Unstructured Play for at Least 90 Minutes**

   Advocate for unstructured playtime and inform about its contribution not only to physical health but also to the development of crucial social skills. Ensure that children engage in a minimum of 90 minutes of play each day, promoting both physical well-being and social interaction. If you reside in an area where accessing a park and making friends is challenging, consider enrolling your child in a sports academy near your home. This provides them with opportunities to socialise, learn new skills, and stay active, all within a convenient location.

4. **Reinforce Fitness Beyond Thinness**

   It is important to emphasise repeatedly that being thin doesn't automatically equate to being fit. Communicate to your child that fitness manifests in various shapes and sizes. Shift discussions about bodies toward topics like stamina, weightlifting, running, and skipping, steering clear of equating fitness solely with thinness.

   Fortunately, we live in an era where conventional beauty standards are continually being questioned and redefined. Fashion models now represent diverse body types, skin tones, and ethnicities, which exposes future generations to a broader understanding of beauty. This increased exposure fosters genuine acceptance and appreciation for the diversity of human appearance.

5. **Redefine Fashion and Self-Esteem**

   Engage in regular conversations about fashion, clothes, and makeup, portraying them as accessories rather than tools for covering up self-esteem. Challenge the influence of brands and societal expectations by occasionally repeating outfits or opting for non-branded attire. Foster self-esteem through discussions on knowledge, experiences, books, and relationships. Encourage diverse interests beyond appearance-related activities.

I clearly remember a moment of pride at a sports shoe store when my children grabbed the model dumbbells, proudly showing off their 'ripped' arms from lifting them. I aspire for my daughters to embrace running in my sneakers with as much enthusiasm as they currently display when walking around the house in my heels.

6. **Celebrate the Body's Functions**

Introduce a body chart to your child, regardless of their age, and discuss the functions of each body part. Promote the idea that the body is beautiful and deserving of acceptance. Keep telling them regularly how each body is a miracle and encourage a positive perception of the body by highlighting its wonderful and awesome capabilities. Include discussions about the brain, emphasising its role in emotions, intelligence, and social skills.

7. **Foster Empathy and Address Bullying**

Teach your child the importance of empathy and discourage them from bullying others based on body size. If your child is a bully, teach them that pointing out someone's shape or size is inappropriate. Address body shaming in a conversation, as discussed in this chapter. If your child is being bullied, provide them with 4 or 5 empathetic responses to stop the bullying. Emphasise that retaliating against a bully isn't helpful. If the bullying persists, ensure your child knows who the safe adults are for them to confide in, such as teachers, older siblings, or parents. Further chapters will delve deeper into strategies for dealing with bullies.

Chapter 6
Personality

In the 19th century, Phineas Gage (1823-60), an American railroad worker, miraculously survived an accident where a large iron rod impaled his skull and destroyed most of his left frontal lobe. This incident resulted in a dramatic personality change, transforming him from a soft-spoken, shy individual into a raging, aggressive, and ill-tempered person overnight.

Personality is a direct reflection of the brain, encompassing intricate higher functions like reasoning, abstraction, concept formation, memories, and emotions. The frontal, temporal, and parietal lobes are key brain regions involved in these processes. Frontal lobe functions include reasoning and abstraction, while the hippocampus and memory network facilitate the formation of new memories. The interaction of these networks with regions regulating temperament and emotion contributes to the development of an individual's personality. It is essential to note that specific personality traits don't originate from distinct brain regions; rather, the brain operates as a complex network.

Psychologists often break down human personality into the 'Big Five' traits: neuroticism (moodiness), extraversion (enthusiasm), openness (open-mindedness), agreeableness (altruism), and conscientiousness (self-control). While these traits offer a general understanding, personality is a multifaceted outcome of genetic and environmental f actors. Trying to categorise individuals into specific boxes is both limiting and impolite. People are often a mix of personalities, and their behaviour can vary based on the environment.

The source of our personality is a fascinating interplay between genetic factors and environmental influences. The age-old debate of nature versus nurture is often explored through scientific studies, with identical twin studies playing a crucial role in unravelling the mystery. Identical twins share identical genetic makeup so their 'nature' component is the same. However, being two distinct individuals undergoing different experiences, the 'nurture their brain receives varies. This makes them valuable subjects for investigating whether personality traits are inherent or shaped by experiences. The most famous and insightful nature vs nurture study involving identical twins is the Minnesota Twin Study, a landmark research effort, studied 350 twins over seven years, including some raised apart. This allowed researchers to assess the relative contributions of heredity and environment to personality development.

In this study, and others like it, identical twins exhibited remarkable similarities in personality, even when raised in different environments. While some twins may show some form of differences, the overall findings suggest a significant genetic influence on personality traits. According to Jerome Kagan, a developmental psychologist at Harvard University, this research is pivotal in understanding personality development, indicating that certain aspects of personality are under considerable genetic control.

Research findings, ranging from the Minnesota study in the 1980s to Richard Plomin's recent book *Blueprint* from the Institute of Psychiatry, Kings College London, consistently suggest that approximately 50 per cent of personality traits are influenced by genetics, with the remaining 50 per cent shaped by environmental factors. This delicate balance underscores the complex and dynamic nature of personality, showcasing both our genetic predispositions and the impact of the world around us.

The significance of this conclusion lies in the nuanced understanding of the interplay between genetics and environment in shaping personality traits. While it might seem obvious that some traits are influenced by genetics and others by environmental factors, delving into the specifics of this 50-50 split reveals the complexity and depth of the neuroscience of personality.

The big science here is in identifying that broad personality traits, such as introversion and agreeableness, have a strong genetic foundation. Research from the University of California, San Diego, led by Dr Chi-Hua Chen, has established links between specific genes and traits like extraversion and neuroticism. This insight challenges the notion that all personality traits are equally malleable and suggests that certain core characteristics are indeed hardwired.

Understanding which part of personality is genetically influenced allows for a more targeted exploration of how these traits manifest. While altering broad personality traits may be challenging, the focus can shift to the more flexible aspects lying beneath the surface. Psychologist Carol Dweck emphasises the malleability of behaviour patterns, habits, and beliefs associated with these broad traits. This distinction opens up avenues for real and lasting changes to certain dimensions of personality, offering a more dynamic perspective on the potential for personal growth and transformation.

1. **Habits**

   Cultivating positive habits is a pivotal avenue for fostering personality change, as habits are learned behaviours that can be reshaped over time. James Clear, in his bestselling book *Atomic Habits*, introduces the 'Thinking, Wanting, Doing, Liking' algorithm, which illustrates how incremental improvements, as small as 1 per cent each day, can lead to substantial changes in personality traits. This groundbreaking book underscores the transformative power of daily habits in shaping long-term personal development.

2. **Beliefs**

   The role of beliefs in shaping personality is paramount. If one holds the belief that change is impossible, the likelihood of initiating change diminishes. Carol Dweck's study with junior high school students experiencing declining math grades exemplifies this. Introducing the concept of the malleability of intelligence, Dweck emphasised that the brain, like any muscle, can strengthen through hard work. Students exposed to this malleable mindset theory exhibited improved math grades and showcased the profound impact of beliefs on motivation and performance.

3. **Mindsets**

   Distinguishing between fixed and malleable mindsets is crucial in understanding how individuals approach challenges. Those with a fixed mindset focus on showcasing innate abilities, often becoming defensive and helpless when faced with setbacks. Conversely, individuals with a malleable mindset prioritise learning and growth, responding to adversity with increased effort and strategic adaptability. This resilience becomes a cornerstone in navigating personal development and overcoming obstacles.

To further understand the significance of these three 'in-betweens' in shaping one's attitude, let's look into an intriguing experiment conducted by Martin Seligman in 1967 at the University of Pennsylvania. In this somewhat cruel yet insightful study, dogs were placed in chambers with a metal base and subjected to mild electric shocks at random intervals. Each chamber was equipped with a switch within the dog's reach, allowing them to stop the shocks if pressed.

Over time, the dogs learned to press the switch promptly upon receiving an electro-shock to prevent further discomfort. In a subsequent experiment, dogs were placed in separate chambers, each receiving mild electric shocks. One chamber had a functional switch to stop the shocks, while the switch in the other chamber was non-functional. The twist lay in the interconnectedness of the switches—pressing the switch in chamber one would halt the shocks in chamber two. However, the dog in chamber two had no control over stopping the shocks directed at them.

Upon returning these dogs from chamber two to their original single chambers that were equipped with switches capable of stopping the shocks, a surprising behaviour emerged. Despite having the means to control the shocks, the dogs refrained from pressing the switch. Having learned from past experiences that they were seemingly incapable of altering their circumstances, they resigned themselves to endure the shocks, exhibiting a classic case of learned helplessness.

This experiment vividly illustrates how the mammalian brain, whether in dogs or humans, tends to relinquish efforts to improve their situation based on past experiences. It highlights the imperative need to instigate change in one or all of the three factors—habit, belief, or mindset—to break free from the shackles of learned helplessness.

Rewards and praise are essential elements in modifying habits, beliefs, and mindsets. They activate the release of dopamine in the brain which is a crucial neurotransmitter which activates the reward pathway in the brain. The outcome is positive reinforcement and motivation. Hence, wanting to convert an introvert into an extrovert may not be the best approach for your child. Instead, help him work to his strengths within the confines of his personality. Shower your child with rewards and praise for his efforts. Motivating him to get into the habit of developing a growth mindset and improving his self-belief may be a better parenting goal. Thus, how we react to experiences hence sets the tone for our attitude towards life. That is why instead of trying to convert your introvert into an extrovert, it's better to help them focus on tweaking their habits, beliefs, and mindset for the better. No matter how much society may be biased towards extrovert people and reward confidence, as a parent it is our duty to make our child feel confident within his own personality and help optimise his/her strengths. In the words of Cheryl Strayed, an American author: 'You don't have a right to the cards you believe you should have been dealt, but you have an obligation to play the hell out of the ones you are holding.'

Effective Strategies for Parents

1. Embrace Positive Thinking for Neuroplasticity

Childhood experiences play a pivotal role in shaping a child's brain, a phenomenon known as neuroplasticity. The brain exhibits changes in response to experiences, with certain areas involved in processing these experiences expanding or forming more synaptic connections (the communication links between nerve cells). To nurture your child's inherent personality, create an environment that fosters positivity, happiness, trust, and minimal stress. This entails avoiding undue panic over minor school grades, refraining from excessive worry over routine falls or mishaps, and steering clear of elevating every issue in your child's life to a life-or-death scenario. By doing so, you contribute to the healthy development of your child's cognitive and emotional well-being.

2. Adopt Child-Centric Parenting

Parenting involves wearing a multitude of hats—tutor, friend, chauffeur, cook, counsellor, and even, according to a toddler, the occasional 'evil witch.' Yet, it is interesting to note how two children growing up in the same household with the same upbringing can develop vastly different personalities. This highlights the complexity of parenting, where not only do parents juggle multiple roles, but they also tailor their approach to accommodate each child's unique traits. For instance, while one of my children thrives with structure and routines, the other flourishes in a more spontaneous and unstructured environment. This means that I need to adopt different strategies to achieve the same goal, such as studying, for each of my children.

It is challenging to fathom how the same parents, home, and environment can give rise to such varied spectrums of personalities. To effectively connect with each child, a parent must metaphorically transform into different personas. Speak as a mentor and coach to the shy, timid child, and adopt the role of a disciplining sergeant for the high-energy, accident-prone one. Child-led parenting, which accommodates and aligns with the child's personality, proves more effective than approaches driven solely by the parents' beliefs and goals. While it might sound akin to a neuro-disorder having multiple personalities within, it is reassuring to know that each person is an amalgamation of 4-5 distinct personality types. So, bring forth the one that resonates with the child conversing with you at any given moment.

3. **Gradual and Consistent Progress**

Transforming habits, beliefs, or mindsets is not an overnight feat—it is not like administering a laxative for instant relief from constipation the next morning. Achieving change requires embracing small, consistent steps. Patience and perseverance are the linchpins. Target minute adjustments in habits, subtle shifts in mindset, or engage in open discussions about any limiting beliefs your child may harbour. Through these incremental changes, pursued daily, you can approach your goal more effectively than through a single attempt.

4. **Commence Today**

Personality traits tend to solidify more as a child transitions into adulthood. The prime window for moulding your child's disposition—whether transforming an introvert into a more outgoing individual or assisting an anxious child in mastering their fears—is during the initial 7-8 years. A concerted focus on personality during this stage can pave the way for smoother teenage years. Parents who typically grapple with academic pressures, homework, and exams might find these concerns alleviated by nurturing motivated and focused kids early on. Ironically, parents often prioritise 'everyday' parenting goals like nutrition, physical development, and safety solely during the first five years. However, it is during these crucial early years that understanding how the brain develops and nurturing it becomes paramount. Investing in personality development during this formative period sets the stage for a teenager who can independently craft admission essays for prestigious institutions like Harvard, without needing constant urging from parents.

5. **Brief Anger Episodes Won't Leave a Lasting Mark**

Parents often fret over the potential long-term effects of expressing anger, be it through yelling, scolding, or other forms of losing one's composure. Young parents often call me panicked about how they vent out on their child and if this would have a lasting effect on his growth. While it is advisable to refrain from such behaviours, it is essential to recognise that a single instance of anger will not cause any form of permanent damage to your child's future happiness. The real concern lies in the consistent repetition of these anger tantrums, which can leave a lasting impact. Childhood trauma typically stems from a prolonged pattern of violent or abusive behaviour, where memories are dominated by recollections of angry and aggressive parents. So, if you had a momentary lapse of anger control recently and find yourself ruminating, grant yourself some compassion—after all, you are only human.

6. Avoid Public Humiliation

A rule I steadfastly adhere to is refraining from humiliating or ridiculing your child in public, irrespective of the gravity of their misbehaviour. If a child throws a tantrum, it is preferable to relocate to a private space for calming down, preventing any form of public chastisement. Similarly, a stage-shy child reluctant to perform can be encouraged to build confidence once back home, without any coercion or ridicule in front of the audience. Psychologists Marte Otten and Kai Jonas from the University of Amsterdam delved into the neural responses of participants exposed to various emotion-inducing scenarios. Their findings highlighted that responses to humiliation were notably more negative, emphasising the detrimental impact of public humiliation. In my opinion, the number one rule for effective parenting is to avoid publicly humiliating your child, regardless of whether the 'public' consists of their 5-year-old friends, your relatives, or strangers.

7. **Within Your Grasp**

Early parenting experiences wield a considerable influence on a child's development. Research by Rohner (1986, 1999) has established robust connections between socialisation practices and personality. Whether within a single culture or across diverse cultures, the acceptance or rejection exhibited by parents significantly shapes their children's personalities. Parents who embrace their children through nurturing actions like hugging and comforting foster sociable, emotionally stable, and self-assured individuals with positive worldviews. Conversely, parents resorting to rejecting behaviours such as hitting, using sarcasm, humiliating, or neglecting may inadvertently contribute to the development of adults characterised by hostility, emotional instability, immature dependency, diminished self-esteem, and a negative worldview. And while it might seem obvious, the truth is that a simple hug given out of love can significantly contribute to shaping your infant's personality. And while it might seem obvious, the truth is that a simple hug given out of love can significantly contribute to shaping your infant's personality.

Practical Tips to Develop Personality

1. **Nurturing Positive Self-Perception**

Kids quickly pick up on cues about whether their parents accept their personality or not. It is concerning to witness parents openly discussing changing their child's personality in front of them. The child may receive signals that being shy is unacceptable. While societal preferences may lean towards extroversion, it doesn't mean that a shy, introverted person is destined for social ridicule.

Consider any example, from Niels Bohr to Bill Gates; all introverted children who excelled in their respective fields. Confidence and self-esteem are independent of extroversion or introversion. Encourage your child to accept themselves and support them in improving habits within the framework of their personality. Avoid expressing dissatisfaction with your child's personality during school meetings or mommy outings, as it may impact their confidence and beliefs about themselves.

2. **Foster Resilience**

   Encourage your children to view failure as a natural part of the learning process. Demonstrate through personal anecdotes or stories of successful individuals that setbacks are not exclusive to certain personality types but are universal experiences that contribute to growth. Instil the idea that coping with stress, maintaining motivation, fostering determination, and embracing positivity are aspects of mindset development, and these qualities can be nurtured in individuals with diverse personality traits. By fostering a mindset that sees challenges as opportunities to learn and improve, children can build resilience and face life's uncertainties with confidence.

3. **Present Parenting**

   By putting away distractions and actively engaging in conversations with your children, you not only demonstrate respect for their opinions but also create a nurturing environment for open communication. This practice helps build trust, as your child learns that their concerns, no matter how small, are valid and valued.

Additionally, being fully present during these interactions allows you to pick up on subtle cues, emotions, and unspoken sentiments, fostering a deeper understanding of your child's experiences. In the long run, this investment in attentive listening lays the foundation for a strong parent-child bond, reinforcing your role as a supportive and understanding presence in their lives. When your child speaks to you, put your phone away, look into their eyes, and listen attentively. It's as simple as that!

4. **Empower through Connection**

   Have you ever noticed how Kate Middleton, the British queen in line, interacts with her kids? Take a moment to look at a photo of her on Google. Notice how she kneels down to be at her child's eye level, speaking to them with one hand on their shoulder or around their waist. It is a simple gesture, yet it speaks volumes about her parenting approach. This small yet impactful act of kneeling down and holding the child not only fosters a sense of emotional security but also encourages your child to express themselves freely. By actively engaging at their eye level, you create a conducive environment for open communication, reinforcing the notion that their thoughts and feelings are not only acknowledged but also respected. Incorporating this practice into your daily interactions contributes to a positive parent-child relationship, where mutual understanding and connection thrive.

5. **Creating Habit-Forming Spaces**

   Creating an environment that aligns with your child's goals is pivotal in instilling positive habits. By minimising distractions and clutter, you enhance their ability to focus on a specific task, laying the groundwork for habit formation. Concentration is particularly crucial for young minds, often prone to wandering. For example, if you aim to cultivate the habit of outdoor play, strategically removing video games, phones, and other toys an hour before the designated playtime significantly boosts the likelihood of your child engaging in outdoor activities with their peers. This intentional approach not only sets the stage for habit development but also teaches valuable lessons about creating conducive environments for personal growth.

6. **Nurture Social Confidence**

   Supporting your introverted child in expanding their social horizons requires a delicate balance. Encourage gradual steps that gently push their boundaries without inducing stress. As a parent, lead by example—initiate conversations with other children in the park, inquire about their interests, and seamlessly introduce them to your child once common ground is discovered. These actions not only provide practical socialising lessons but also illustrate to your child that friendships can be cultivated in a relaxed and authentic manner, fostering a sense of ease in social situations.

7. **Build Self-Assurance**

   Empower your child's growing sense of self by actively seeking their input on everyday matters. While they are in the process of maturing, treating them with respect and valuing their opinions contributes significantly to shaping their emerging personality. Demonstrating that their thoughts and viewpoints matter fosters a sense of importance and autonomy, laying the groundwork for a confident and self-assured individual. As a parent, recognising and appreciating their perspective in decision-making not only boosts their self-esteem but also cultivates a healthy parent-child dynamic based on trust and mutual respect.

A simple yet effective way to begin fostering independence is by involving your child in the decision-making process. For instance, you can ask for their opinion on what you should wear for an upcoming party. Show them 3-4 options you have in mind and let them pick what you wear. This small gesture not only boosts their confidence but also reinforces the idea that their opinions matter.

8. Empower Boundaries

Instilling the significance of saying 'No' in a polite yet firm manner is a valuable life lesson. Demonstrate to your child that strength of personality and character hold more weight than physical or vocal dominance. Emphasise that expressing a firm stance doesn't mean resorting to physical or vocal strength. Teaching this distinction early on equips children with crucial tools for navigating boundaries and asserting themselves in various situations. By fostering a mindset where assertiveness is rooted in respect and self-assurance, you contribute to the development of a confident and resilient individual capable of navigating interpersonal dynamics with grace and integrity.

This trait can be particularly challenging for parents to display consistently. However, it's crucial to maintain firmness in your decisions, especially when faced with persistent requests from your child. In situations like the 'Asking loop,' where your child repeatedly asks for something you have declined, such as having soda at a party, it is important to stick to your stance politely. Even if your child asks 24 times, respond calmly and firmly with a simple 'No' each time. By doing so, you not only prevent your child from consuming unhealthy soda but also teach them the value of standing firm without resorting to anger or aggression.

9. Cultivate Global Perspectives

Inspire your child's sense of curiosity and adventure by encouraging them to travel and explore the world beyond their immediate surroundings. Travelling provides a unique opportunity for exposure to diverse cultures, viewpoints, opinions, and experiences, contributing significantly to the shaping of their personality from a young age. Children who have ventured into various places tend to exhibit qualities of acceptance, resilience, and a heightened comfort with themselves. Opting for destinations that are markedly different from your usual residence not only broadens their horizons but also fosters adaptability and an appreciation for diversity. The transformative impact of travel on a child's development extends beyond the excitement of new landscapes; it lays the groundwork for a well-rounded individual with a global perspective and an open mind.

10. Promote Inner Strength

Show your children that true confidence stems from inner qualities rather than external factors such as clothing, gadgets, or possessions. By emphasising that genuine confidence is anchored in personality and self-worth, you equip them with a foundation that remains unwavering. Unlike external elements that are subject to change over time, internal qualities endure. Instil the understanding that their character, kindness, resilience, and determination are the true sources of self-assurance. By fostering a sense of confidence grounded in intrinsic values, you empower your children to navigate life's challenges with authenticity and resilience, promoting lasting self-esteem irrespective of external circumstances.

11. Build Self-Reliance

Resist the urge to swoop in and solve every challenge your child encounters, as this tendency can inadvertently diminish their self-esteem. The phenomenon known as helicopter parenting, prevalent in the millennial generation, has been linked to hindering crucial learning experiences and leading to 'learned helplessness' in children. Providing space for your child to navigate challenges independently not only cultivates resilience but also nurtures crucial problem-solving skills. By allowing them to grapple with difficulties, make decisions, and find solutions, you instil a sense of autonomy and capability that becomes foundational to their self-esteem. This approach encourages a healthy sense of self-reliance, teaching them that overcoming obstacles is an integral part of personal growth and development.

10. Promote Inner Strength

Show your children that true confidence stems from inner qualities rather than external factors such as clothing, gadgets, or possessions. By emphasising that genuine confidence is anchored in personality and self-worth, you equip them with a foundation that remains unwavering. Unlike external elements that are subject to change over time, internal qualities endure. Instil the understanding that their character, kindness, resilience, and determination are the true sources of self-assurance. In fostering a sense of confidence grounded in intrinsic values, you empower your children to navigate life's challenges with authenticity and resilience, promoting lasting self-esteem irrespective of external circumstances.

11. Build Self-Reliance

Resist the urge to swoop in and solve every challenge your child encounters, as this tendency can inadvertently diminish their self-esteem. The phenomenon known as helicopter parenting, prevalent in the millennial generation, has been linked to hindering crucial learning experiences and leading to ill-armed helplessness in children. Providing space for your child to navigate challenges independently not only cultivates resilience but also nurtures crucial problem-solving skills. By allowing them to grapple with difficulties, make decisions, and find solutions, you instil a sense of autonomy and capability that becomes foundational to their self-esteem. This approach encourages a healthy sense of self-reliance, teaching them that overcoming obstacles is an integral part of personal growth and development.

Chapter 7

Peer Pressure

Peer pressure often serves as the scapegoat for justifying many actions, whether by children or adults. For instance, our child might demand an iPhone because their friend has one, or we might find ourselves splurging on unnecessary items during a shopping spree with friends simply because everyone else is doing the same. These scenarios vividly illustrate how much our behaviour is influenced by those around us, regardless of age. Perhaps this is what Aesop meant when he said, 'A man is known by the company he keeps.' Modern motivational speaker, Jim Rohn, further emphasises this concept, suggesting that we become the average of the five people we spend the most time with. However, instead of immediately scrutinising our friends, let's redirect the focus of peer pressure from our social circles to our brains, where all the magic (or voodoo) happens!

Surprisingly, numerous intriguing experiments have been conducted on peer pressure. This interest likely stems from the fact that peer pressure affects nearly every human being, and we all aspire to overcome it. And to transcend peer pressure, the first step is understanding why it occurs. Scientists refer to this area of research as the science of social influence and social conformity.

One of the most notable experiments shedding light on social conformity dates back to the 1950s and was conducted by Solomon Asch. In this experiment, Asch assembled a group of eight students and presented them with a seemingly straightforward task: to determine which of three lines matched a standard line in length. At first glance, the correct answer was obvious—line 2. However, the twist in the experiment lay in the fact that out of the eight participants, only one was a genuine participant. The rest were instructed to intentionally provide incorrect answers. Unaware of this setup, the real participant believed that the other seven individuals were fellow participants like themselves. Compounding the pressure, the real participant was always seated at the end of the row and asked to give their answer last. Asch conducted 12 critical trials under these conditions.

Surprisingly, in about 75 per cent of the critical trials, participants chose to go along with the group's incorrect answer, despite the obviousness of the correct choice. Strikingly, when participants were asked to complete the task in private, none of them gave the wrong answer. This phenomenon suggests that individuals often prioritise fitting in with the group over trusting their own judgement and intelligence, particularly in a social setting.

Asch's experiment offers valuable insights into the dynamics of group behaviour and sheds light on phenomena like mob mentality. It helps explain how individuals may engage in actions they wouldn't normally condone or consider, simply to conform to group norms and expectations. This phenomenon extends beyond extreme cases like communal violence to everyday situations where individuals may compromise their values to align with group behaviour, such as participating in bullying to fit in with peers.

So, let's now consider the following questions: Why do people often succumb to negative behaviour just because others are doing it? Would we feel pressured to be kind if we were surrounded by a group of individuals practising yoga, meditating, studying, and working hard? Or does peer pressure exclusively exert a negative influence?

Based on Asch's line experiment, the answer to these questions boils down to the brain's innate tendency to seek acceptance and belonging. Participants in Asch's experiments admitted that they gave wrong answers to avoid standing out and facing ridicule or persecution for being different.

While some, like British social psychologist John Turner, have raised doubts about Asch's conformity experiments, modern studies suggest that today's students exhibit more confidence and are more likely to stick to obvious correct answers compared to those in the 1950s. However, even if cultural factors have contributed to this shift, recent experiments indicate that individuals continue to be influenced by social dynamics, whether consciously or unconsciously. Thus, understanding who influences us and how they do so hold the key to addressing peer pressure issues, particularly among children. By unravelling these influences, we may uncover strategies to empower individuals to resist negative peer pressure and make independent decisions.

The trial of German Nazi war criminal Adolf Eichmann in Jerusalem remains a deeply unsettling chapter in human history. Just days before his execution, Eichmann penned a plea for clemency to the Israeli President, arguing that he should not be held accountable for the Holocaust as he was simply following orders. He brazenly claimed he felt no guilt and portrayed himself as a mere pawn in the grand scheme of things. However, this plea reeked of delusion, given Eichmann's pivotal role in orchestrating the genocide and facilitating the mass transportation of Jews to extermination camps.

Eichmann's case serves as a stark reminder of how individuals can justify abhorrent actions when commanded by authority figures, as was the case with Hitler. This phenomenon of blind obedience to authority figures was further explored in an experiment conducted by Stanley Milgram of Yale University. Milgram's experiment involved three roles: an experimenter (E), a learner (L), and a teacher (T). The teacher was instructed to administer increasingly intense electric shocks to the learner whenever they answered a question incorrectly. Unbeknownst to the teacher, the shocks were fake, and the learner was merely acting out their responses. Despite the learner's apparent distress, many participants continued to administer shocks, even up to levels labelled as lethal.

This chilling experiment revealed the disturbing capacity within each of us to obey authority figures, even when it conflicts with our moral compass. Eichmann's plea for clemency and Milgram's experiment shed light on the complex interplay between obedience, authority, and individual responsibility in the face of morally reprehensible acts.

Would an ordinary person administer electric shocks to another individual simply because a scientist in authority instructed them to do so? Do everyday individuals harbour latent tendencies akin to those exhibited by notorious figures like Eichmann? The findings from the actual experiments proved to be profoundly startling.

Astonishingly, approximately 65 per cent of participants persisted in administering shocks to the learner, escalating to the maximum of 450 volts, despite warnings indicating the shock's severity. This alarming behaviour unfolded within the context of what was purported to be a learning experiment.

Did the temporal context of Milgram's experiment in the 1960s exert a similar cultural influence as Asch's experiments? Replications of Milgram's experiments conducted in 2009 by Dr Jerry Burger of Santa Clara University yielded comparable results, although with a maximum shock level of 150 volts. While participants weren't led to believe they were committing murder, the study underscored that even in 2009, individuals were willing to deliver electric shocks to others simply because a figure of authority (the scientist) instructed them to do so.

In essence, humans display a tendency to conform to or appease individuals whom they perceive as wielding power over them. In such scenarios, personal ethics often take a backseat as individuals rationalise their actions to themselves. Therefore, it is important to note that power manifests in various forms. One of the most influential theories on power was developed by Bertram Raven and John French, who identified five distinct types of power:

Reward Power

This type of power operates on the principle of obedience in exchange for rewards. For instance, individuals may comply with someone's directives in hopes of gaining social acceptance, such as befriending the coolest kid in class to boost their own popularity.

1. **Coercive Power**

   Here, obedience stems from the fear of punishment. An example of coercive power in action is when a child bullies another peer to avoid becoming a target of ridicule from their own group of friends.

2. **Legitimate power**

   Obedience is driven by the belief that the person in authority has the right to demand compliance. This could manifest in scenarios where individuals adhere to the instructions of a teacher or a judge due to their recognised authority.

3. **Referent Power**

   This type of power involves obeying someone whom we admire or respect as an influential figure. For instance, a young teenager might engage in reckless behaviour to impress a crush, while others might blindly follow a charismatic leader despite allegations against them, as seen in the case of religious cult leaders.

4. **Expert Power**

   Obedience is directed towards individuals perceived to possess superior knowledge or expertise in a particular field. This could involve seeking medical advice from a qualified doctor or, in more concerning situations, relying on misguided advice from peers who claim expertise, such as a self-proclaimed 'sex expert' among teenagers.

Any parent can relate to the influence of these power figures within their child's social circle. We have learnt from the science of social influence that individuals often succumb to peer pressure due to the brain's inherent desire for acceptance and conformity. This innate need to belong can lead us to comply with unjust demands, even if they conflict with our personal moral beliefs. But how can we leverage this understanding of social influence to protect our children from negative peer pressure and equip them with the ability to make sound decisions in social settings? Is there a scientific approach that offers guidance on navigating this common challenge in parenting?

In short, yes. To understand this better, let's examine some objective research.

Curter-Smith and Lewis conducted a study in 1994, which gathered data from forty-one mothers and their adolescent sons through face-to-face interviews and follow-up telephone interviews. They found that adolescents most susceptible to anti-social peer pressure often perceived low levels of fatherly monitoring. Additionally, these adolescents tended to experience inappropriate discipline from their fathers and were raised in households with mothers who practised an authoritarian parenting style, even after controlling for the adolescents' anti-social values.

Further insights come from Tomas Paus and his colleagues at the University of Nottingham's Brain and Body Centre. In their 2007 study published in the *Journal of Neuroscience* titled, 'Neural Mechanisms of Resistance to Peer Influence in Early Adolescence,' they examined neural correlates associated with the ability to resist peer pressure. Forty-six 10-year-olds participated in the study, completing a carefully designed questionnaire. The findings revealed that children who exhibited high resistance to peer pressure showed increased activity in the prefrontal cortex, a brain region crucial for decision-making and inhibiting unwanted behaviour. Additionally, these peer-resistant children demonstrated stronger connections between brain regions involved in perceiving social cues and planning behaviour.

To delve into the early roots of peer pressure, Smith and Fowler conducted a study involving eight kindergarten children, aged 5 to 7, who had been referred for behaviour management and academic support by parents or school personnel due to disruptive behaviour in their regular classroom. These children exhibited behaviours that interfered with their performance in the kindergarten setting. While the entire class participated in all phases of the study, observational data were specifically collected for three children (C1, C2, C3) identified by the classroom teacher as the most disruptive.

In the first experiment, rewards and punishment tokens were distributed by teachers, while in the second experiment, classroom peers were tasked with introducing and overseeing the token system without prior teacher supervision. The aim was to determine if peers could effectively manage the token system. Results from both experiments revealed that kindergarten-aged children with behaviour and learning challenges could successfully influence the behaviour of their peers. This study demonstrated that children can both effectively manage their peers' behaviour and be influenced by their peers. These studies provide insights into three key strategies for building resistance to peer pressure and anti-social behaviour in children.

Here are three crucial strategies to foster resilience against peer pressure and anti-social behaviour in children:

1. **Emotionally Engaged Parenting**

   Research suggests that children benefit from active involvement from both parents in their upbringing. Out of the four broadly categorised parenting styles, authoritative parenting is most suited for the millennial scenario. The other three styles are permissive parenting, uninvolved parenting, and authoritarian parenting. While authoritarian parenting doles out punishment for discipline, authoritative parenting enforces rules and discipline in a more nurturing guided manner. Thus, it is essential for parents to adopt an authoritative parenting style and strike a balance between authoritarian and permissive approaches. Authoritative parents are both nurturing and firm, which provides the child support and guidance while also enforcing fair and consistent discipline and boundaries. The aspect of politeness coupled with firmness has been emphasised earlier in this book as well.

2. **Promote Independence and Decision-Making Skills**

   Encourage children to develop independence and the ability to make reasoned decisions from a young age. Teach them that every decision, whether positive or negative, has consequences, and help them learn to face these consequences with courage and humility.

   Indian parents are often associated with instilling discipline, yet the process typically begins quite late. However, the optimal time to teach independent decision-making skills is actually before the age of seven. By this age, a child's brain is still highly receptive to learning and forming habits. Moreover, the consequences of mistakes made during this period are generally not life-threatening, making it an ideal time for experiential learning. For instance, allowing a three-year-old to climb a small step stool provides a safe opportunity for them to learn from any minor falls, reinforcing the connection between actions and consequences in their developing brain. Therefore, this process of skill-building should commence in toddlerhood to instil resilience before the challenges of adolescence arise.

3. **Harness Positive Peer Influence**

   Recognise the impact peers can have on children's behaviour and use it to their advantage. Encourage positive peer interactions by ensuring that your child surrounds themselves with friends who inspire and motivate them to excel. Be mindful of the company your child keeps, ensuring that their closest friends encourage them to set high standards and make positive choices. Also, do not let academic proficiency, religion, caste, or any other such criteria limit your child's friendships. The most important factor should be whether your child's friend is happy, positive, and friendly.

Effective Strategies for Parents

1. **Listen Attentively**

   It is easy to dismiss our children's concerns or requests without truly hearing them out. However, taking the time to listen to their entire story, even if you know you will ultimately say no, is crucial. Giving them the opportunity to express themselves fully instils a sense of validation and assurance. Often, allowing your child to finish their story or request before dismissing it outrightly can make them feel heard. In the event that you do decide to dismiss the plea, it is often met with less resistance or protest. So, let them make their case, even if you are already inclined to decline. Being heard is immensely empowering for children.

2. **Use 'No' Wisely**

   While it is important to listen and consider your child's requests, it is equally important to assert boundaries when necessary. Rather than saying no to every demand, use your negative responses sparingly but firmly. As I mentioned in my book, *100 Ways to be a Stress-Free Mom and Raise Happy Kids,* not every request warrants an outright rejection. However, when you do say no, stand your ground, regardless of any pressure or attempts at manipulation from your child. Teaching them the significance of a firm 'no' early on helps them navigate more significant challenges like peer pressure, substance abuse, and other social issues with confidence and resilience.

3. **Establish Clear Ground Rules**

   Providing children with clear guidelines from the outset helps them understand what's acceptable and what's not. For instance, implementing a rule like allowing two toys per month (or any other reasonable limit) sets a clear boundary for toy purchases. This allows children to plan their acquisitions in advance and fosters a sense of responsibility. As children grow into their teenage years, it is beneficial to engage them in discussions about ground rules. By involving them in rule-making, they gain a deeper understanding of the family's expectations and boundaries. Additionally, it is important to periodically revisit and adjust these rules as children mature.

4. **Lead by Example**

Children often emulate the behaviour they observe in their parents. This rings especially true in today's materialistic society. If parents constantly talk about the materialistic possessions of others, such as the latest iPhone or extravagant clothing, children are likely to develop a similar mindset of comparison and materialism. Therefore, it is vital for parents to be mindful of their conversations about material possessions in front of their children. While achieving milestones like purchasing a luxury car may be celebrated, the focus should be on the values of hard work, gratitude, and perseverance rather than flaunting material wealth on social media platforms. By modelling humility and gratitude, parents can instil more meaningful values in their children.

5. **Avoid Using Blackmail**

How often do we resort to bribing or threatening our children to get them to do what we want? Whether it is persuading them to finish their meals or manipulating them with promises of rewards, we inadvertently teach them the same tactics. Instead, let's limit our use of blackmail and opt for clear communication. For example, rather than saying, 'Eat your food or you won't get dessert,' simply state, 'It is important to finish your meal.' By allowing children to experience the natural consequences of their actions, such as not studying and facing the outcomes, they learn valuable lessons that prepare them for future successes.

Practical Tips to Tackle Peer Pressure

1. Hear Them Out

Peer pressure affects everyone, including our children. When your child starts expressing envy or frustration about what their friends have, it is essential not to brush off their feelings. Whether it is about lacking the latest gadgets, not going on extravagant trips, or feeling left out for not having experienced certain things, these concerns are valid to them. Instead of dismissing their emotions, consider it a blessing that your child feels comfortable confiding in you. Encourage open communication by letting them know that sharing their experiences is always welcome. This creates a supportive environment where they feel understood and can seek guidance when navigating peer influence. So, next time, listen to your child as she excitedly shares news about her friend's latest PSP. Engage her with follow-up questions such as, 'What features does the new PSP offer compared to the older version?', 'What makes owning a PSP so thrilling?', and 'If someone couldn't afford a PSP, what alternatives could they explore?' These inquiries prompt your child to contemplate peer influence critically, moving beyond simply following the crowd. Remember, acknowledging their feelings is the first step toward helping them develop resilience and confidence in the face of peer pressure.

2. **Encourage Exploration of Alternative Options**

   Empower your child by presenting them with alternative options and solutions. Instead of simply listing off what they shouldn't do, focus on providing constructive alternatives. Encourage them to explore different paths and possibilities. By offering viable alternatives, you equip your child with the tools they need to make informed decisions and navigate peer pressure effectively. This approach not only fosters critical thinking skills but also empowers them to take control of their choices as well as strengthens their ability to resist negative influences.

3. **Cultivate Clarity and Values**

   In today's rapidly changing world, characterised by shifting moralities, evolving ideals, and diverse societal norms, children often find themselves grappling with confusion and uncertainty. In such a complex landscape, it is crucial to provide them with clarity and guidance. For instance, there are numerous social causes in today's world that individuals can actively support. And since humans naturally gravitate towards being associated with noble endeavours, such social issues provide ideal opportunities for children to develop empathy, compassion, and a sense of social responsibility. Additionally, being part of a family that stands for something significant instils a sense of confidence in the child that extends beyond mere material possessions. Unfortunately, many adults themselves struggle to define their beliefs and values. A proactive approach involves engaging in regular conversations with your children, ideally once a week, to explore and define the social causes your family stands for, identify important ethical principles, and establish clear boundaries. These discussions lay the groundwork for emotional well-being, which is especially critical during the formative years. For example, our household has embraced a plastic-free lifestyle, recently replacing our last plastic item with bamboo brushes. Witnessing this shift, my kids now take immense pride in our family's efforts to contribute to a healthier planet.

4. **Priorities Brain Education for Holistic Development**

   Our understanding of the brain often receives inadequate attention compared to other bodily organs. While we may be well-versed in the functions of the heart, lungs, and digestive system, the intricacies of the brain and cognition remain largely unexplored. Ironically, educating children about brain function, emotions, sibling dynamics, and the influence of peers is integral to cognitive development. Thus, it is essential for parents to invest time in learning about the basics of brain function and cognition. By incorporating brain education into our parenting approach, we empower children to better understand themselves, navigate social interactions, and foster emotional intelligence. Additionally, understanding how the brain functions can shield you from being lured into purchasing excessively expensive toys and courses that promise brain development without any scientific backing!

5. **Encouraging Thoughtful Emotional Responses**

   It is common for people to act impulsively based on their emotions without considering the logical consequences.

To instil better decision-making skills, teach your children to take a moment to analyse their feelings before reacting. Instead of simply reacting to emotions, encourage them to pause and think through their response logically. By introducing this small but crucial step, children can learn to navigate their emotions more effectively and make informed decisions. Additionally, provide them with examples of how thinking before reacting can lead to better outcomes in various situations. Emphasise the importance of considering the consequences of their actions and how taking a moment to think can prevent unnecessary conflicts or regrets. This practice not only helps them develop emotional intelligence but also fosters a sense of responsibility and maturity in handling challenging emotions.

6. Navigating Digital Parental Controls for Safer Online Experiences

In today's digital age, children are exposed to unprecedented levels of peer pressure due to the widespread use of technology. Social media and the internet have become constant companions, making it easier for peer pressure to infiltrate every aspect of a child's life. Another major concern with the digital landscape is the prevalence of online bullying, or trolling, which thrives on anonymity. Without adequate parental controls in place, children can easily fall victim to cyberbullying without their parents even being aware of it. Moreover, many parents overlook the importance of using age-appropriate media and implementing parental control apps on their devices. Platforms like Facebook have age restrictions in place, yet underage children often find ways to bypass these restrictions and create accounts. Similarly, email services like Gmail allow minors to have accounts only if they are linked to their parents' email accounts, but this requirement is often ignored.

Given these challenges, it is essential for parents to educate themselves about digital technology, its potential risks, and the importance of implementing parental controls. By limiting their children's exposure to social media and monitoring their online activities, parents can create a safer online environment for their children and mitigate the negative effects of peer pressure in the digital realm. For more in-depth insights into managing screen time and practical tips to handle it effectively, kindly refer to the dedicated chapter on screen time management in this book.

7. Harnessing the Power of Positive Peer Pressure

Peer pressure is a potent force in shaping your child's behaviour and choices. Instead of viewing it solely as a negative influence, consider leveraging peer pressure in a positive way to encourage desirable behaviours and attitudes. Encourage your child to surround themselves with friends who embody the values and behaviours you want to promote. Positive peer pressure can motivate your child to excel academically, participate in extracurricular activities, and make healthier lifestyle choices. Identify a core hobby that your child is passionate about, such as reading, drawing, or athletics. Encourage your child to spend time pursuing these hobbies with friends who share similar interests from their circle. This promotes a sense of camaraderie and enjoyment in their shared activities. Moreover, by fostering a supportive peer group, you create an environment where children uplift and inspire each other to reach their full potential.

8. **Embrace the Strength of Empathy**

   In a world that often praises toughness and stoicism, it is important to highlight the strength and value of empathy. Encourage your child to recognise that being kind, compassionate, and understanding are not signs of weakness, but rather qualities that demonstrate courage and integrity. Share stories with your child that illustrate the power of empathy in overcoming challenges and building meaningful relationships. Show them examples of individuals who have achieved success and fulfilment by embracing empathy in their interactions with others. Also incorporate activities that nurture empathy into your family's routine. Whether it's volunteering at a local charity, participating in acts of kindness, or engaging in discussions about empathy and compassion, these experiences can help cultivate a deeper understanding of the importance of empathy in our lives.

9. **Get to Know Your Child's Friends and Their Families**

   Understanding your child's social circle is crucial, as friends wield significant influence outside the home. Take the time to learn about your child's friends, their backgrounds, and the values they uphold. Building relationships with the parents of your child's friends can provide valuable insights into their family dynamics and the messages being communicated within their households. By fostering open communication with other parents, you can exchange perspectives on parenting styles, values, and expectations. This collaboration creates a supportive network where you can share concerns, address common challenges, and work together to promote positive development in your children. Ultimately, by actively engaging with your child's social circle, you can help shape a supportive and enriching environment that fosters healthy friendships and reinforces the values you wish to instil in your child.

Chapter 8

Bullying and Racism

In scientific literature, terms such as 'bullying' or 'peer victimisation' are commonly used to describe aggressive behaviour that is repeated over time. A 2017 survey conducted by The Teachers Foundation and Wipro Applying Thought In School (WATIS) across 15 cities in India found that 42 per cent of students in Classes 4 to 8 and 36 per cent in Classes 9 to 12 reported experiencing harassment by peers on school campuses. Bullying can leave both physical and emotional scars and poses significant burdens on young children with developing brains.

While bullying has often been viewed as a childhood rite of passage, recent scientific evidence highlights its detrimental effects on emotional, physical, and mental well-being, both for the bully and the victim. It extends beyond mere growing pains, potentially leading to long-term changes in the brain that result in cognitive and emotional deficits comparable to those caused by child abuse.

Chronic stress is a known risk factor for substance abuse. In the light of this, Klaus Miczek at Tufts University conducted a study to investigate whether being a victim of bullying carries similar risks. To simulate bullying in rodents, Miczek introduced an older, more aggressive rat or mouse into the cage of a juvenile animal. The dominant animal exhibited behaviours such as pushing or even biting the younger one to assert dominance. Upon studying the brains of the bullied animals, Miczek found elevated levels of the stress hormone corticosterone in certain brain areas, with traces of the hormone persisting long after the stressor had ceased. Remarkably, when given access to drugs like cocaine and alcohol, the bullied rodents consumed more of these substances compared to their non-bullied counterparts, even months later into adulthood.

The important question to consider here is whether these findings be extrapolated to humans? Tracy Vaillancourt, a psychologist at the University of Ottawa, discovered that bullied boys and girls exhibit abnormal levels of cortisol compared to their non-bullied peers. In these children, abnormal cortisol levels can weaken the immune system and even lead to the death of nerve cells in the hippocampus, a brain region crucial for memory. As a result, bullied children face elevated risks of substance abuse, academic struggles, and poor performance on standardised tests. Moreover, they are more likely to develop impulsive and aggressive behaviours as teenagers, perpetuating the cycle of bullying.

Bullying exerts such a profound influence on a child's development that it can induce permanent and irreversible changes in the brain. What insights can neuroanatomical studies provide on bullying? The anterior cingulate gyrus, a brain region responsible for two key functions related to bullying, is worth examining. Firstly, it triggers our fear response; for instance, if a child is pushed on the playground and feels threatened, this part of the brain becomes hyperactive. Secondly, it plays a pivotal role in our capacity for empathy. This highlights the importance, in a bullying scenario, of either trying to understand the perspective of the bully or learning social norms and boundaries.

It is vital to consider that the regions of the brain responsible for empathy are undergoing changes in today's teenagers. A study led by Sara H. Konrath from the Institute of Social Research, involving approximately 13,000 college students, revealed a startling trend: young people today exhibit 40 per cent lower levels of empathy compared to students in the 1970s. This decline in empathy underscores the prevalence of issues like bullying and other millennial challenges rooted in emotional health. Researcher Martin Teicher's findings further shed light on the impact of childhood experiences on brain development. He discovered that the corpus callosums of children who have suffered child abuse are, on average, 40 per cent smaller. This reduction in neural connectivity can manifest in manic mood shifts, difficulties in social intelligence, and challenges in processing the surrounding environment for teens.

Notably, the brains of bullies themselves are also affected. Dr Carlisi from University College London conducted MRI scans on 672 individuals in 2019, including lifelong anti-social individuals who exhibited bullying behaviours from childhood into adulthood, as well as those who reformed later in life. The MRI scans revealed that lifelong bullies had thinner cortex, areas crucial for rational decision-making, and lower total brain surface areas. Conversely, those who reformed as adults displayed brain structures comparable to individuals who had never engaged in bullying behaviour. These findings underscore the profound impact of both early experiences and behaviour patterns on brain development and function.

Just like in other aspects of child development, emotional intelligence (EI) plays a pivotal role in understanding and addressing bullying. EI encompasses the ability to perceive, understand, and manage emotions, both in oneself and others by combining emotional and intellectual processes. Lower emotional intelligence appears to correlate with involvement in bullying, whether as the bully or the victim. Understanding and managing one's emotions is crucial in preventing children from engaging in bullying behaviour and can also help prevent victims from becoming bullies later in life. This underscores the importance of integrating EI and social skills into everyday parenting practices.

Anthropologists and evolutionary scientists propose that bullying may stem from a social need to establish hierarchies among peers. Humans, as social animals, are wired to establish social hierarchies in their interactions. Those seeking control or power may resort to bullying, often interacting with others only on their terms, and use aggression when things don't go their way. Additionally, athletes and physically strong students may engage in bullying due to the power they hold over weaker peers. However, bullying isn't solely about power; it can also be driven by a desire for popularity. It has been seen that popular children sometimes perpetuate aggression through gossip or rumours to maintain their status in the social hierarchy.

Issues surrounding bullying often originate within the home environment. Children from abusive households are more prone to bullying, as they may perceive aggression and violence as common solutions due to what they witness at home. Similarly, children with permissive or absent parents may resort to bullying as a means of gaining a sense of power and control that they lack in their own lives, seeking attention that ideally should come from a parent or caregiver.

It is also a misconception that only physically weaker children are targets of bullying. The fact is that being different in any way can also make one susceptible to bullying. Teens often target their peers for their differences, such as having special needs or food allergies or being of a different race, religion, or sexual orientation. Prejudice is often at the root of such bullying incidents. For instance, Nazia Erum's book *Mothering a Muslim: The Dark Secrets in Our Schools and Playgrounds* sheds light on racial discrimination against minority children. News headlines frequently report instances of verbal or physical abuse against students from North-East India in places like Delhi University, reflecting prevalent discrimination based on ethnicity. Discrimination based on skin colour is rampant even in progressive Western societies, and in India, matrimonial advertisements seeking a 'fair' bride perpetuate this form of bullying, leading to peer victimisation. While bullying may be carried out by individual children, its perpetuation involves larger spheres of influence including family dynamics, societal norms, and media portrayals.

In the modern era, a new form of bullying has emerged: cyberbullying. This form of harassment or bullying occurs through digital devices such as computers, smartphones, and tablets. While the hurt and humiliation experienced by victims are similar to other forms of bullying, the reach of cyberbullying extends into every home due to the internet's global accessibility, making it potentially more difficult to manage and contain. In 2018, India recorded the highest rate of children falling victim to cyberbullying, according to a survey conducted in 28 countries by the UK-based consumer tech review firm Comparitech.

Cyberbullying can occur across various online platforms, including social media, chat rooms, and gaming platforms, where individuals can view and participate in the sharing of content. Common types of cyberbullying involve humiliating individuals through hateful comments on online platforms or through SMS or messaging. This includes posting, sending, or sharing negative, nasty, or false information about another individual with the intent to cause humiliation and character assassination. Recognising the severity of the issue, the Ministry of Women and Child Development in India has launched a dedicated helpline (complaint-mwcd@gov.in) for reporting cyberbullying, online harassment, and cyber defamation, particularly targeting women and children. Cyberbullying, along with cyberstalking and paedophilia, constitutes a significant aspect of cybercrime. It is alarming how easily young, impressionable children can fall prey to online predators who masquerade as harmless friends on social media platforms, chat rooms, or online gaming sites. To address the security concerns associated with children's screen usage, please refer to the discussion in Chapter 1.

Effective Strategies for Parents

1. Monitor Your Child's Behavior

Bullying often targets young kids who are still learning to navigate their emotions. Victims frequently retreat into silence as they grapple with the situation and often blame themselves due to the stigma associated with being bullied. This can severely hinder their ability to communicate with trusted adults, caregivers, or parents. If you observe sudden shifts in your child's behaviour, it is essential to initiate conversations with them, their peers, other parents in the community, and even school staff.

2. **Teach Empathy and Equality**

   It is important to instil in our children the understanding that all living beings are equal. Whether it is a cat or a human, each life has its value, formed through intricate processes of evolution and spirituality. By fostering empathy towards all creatures from a young age, we can work towards eradicating hate from our society. The divisive politics fuelled by hate exists because there are individuals who endorse it. As parents, we wield the influence and power to halt the transmission of hatred from one generation to the next.

3. **Teach Your Child About Choice**

   If you discover that your child is displaying bullying behaviour, then make sure to not respond with self-pity or aggression. Instead, take the opportunity to educate them about the concepts of choice, consent, and respect. Choice is a personal decision, allowing individuals to select according to their preferences or beliefs. Teaching the importance of consent is paramount in today's world. It entails having the option to say yes or no, which lays the foundation for empathy. Every child should learn to assertively say no if they experience bullying, as well as to respect the boundaries and choices of others.

4. **Foster Kindness as a Fundamental Value**

   Intelligence doesn't always correlate with kindness, as illustrated by a personal anecdote of a highly intelligent student who tended to be unkind to his peers. In my experience as a parent coach, I have encountered situations where the most academically gifted child turns out to be the class bully. It's a common scenario. In such cases, I always advise parents to prioritise lessons in kindness alongside academic success. While it is natural to feel proud of your child's achievements, it is equally important to nurture empathy and compassion. Engaging in a simple conversation like, 'Being clever is a gift, but kindness is a skill we must all learn. If you excel in learning, ensure that kindness is your first lesson,' can make a significant impact. Therefore, instilling this value in our children is crucial for their overall development.

5. **Create an Open Channel for Reporting Discrimination**

   While immediate solutions to our children's problems may not always be at hand, being a supportive listener can profoundly impact their well-being. Create a safe harbour where your children feel empowered to share any experiences of discrimination or bullying they face. This open line of communication fosters trust and reassurance, ensuring that they know they are not alone in facing challenges. Encourage them to express their feelings and concerns openly and assure them that you are there to offer support and guidance whenever needed. By actively listening and empathising with their struggles, you can provide invaluable emotional support and help them navigate difficult situations with resilience and confidence.

6. **Teach Effective Responses to Discrimination**
   Discrimination cannot be combated with a tit-for-tat mentality. When faced with mockery or prejudice based on factors like skin colour, caste, religion, or beliefs, encourage your child to respond with empathy and understanding. Instead of retaliating, teach them to assert their position calmly and also emphasise that differing perspectives don't make either party wrong or right. Aim to foster understanding and compassion, as love is the antidote to hate.

7. **Encourage Selective Hearing**
   In my previous book, *100 Ways to Be a Stress-Free Mom and Raise Happy Kids*, I shared a chapter titled 'Build a Mental Blind Spot.' This concept highlights the importance of filtering out unsolicited advice and criticism to maintain peace of mind. Just as parents learn to overlook certain things to reduce stress, children can benefit from developing a similar skill. Teach your children to discern which battles are worth fighting and when it's best to simply walk away. Not everything warrants a reaction, and not everyone deserves their time and energy. By mastering the art of selective hearing, children can conserve their mental and emotional resources for what truly matters.

Practical Tips to Deal with Bullying

1. **Break the Cycle**
   Avoid escalating conflicts by retaliating with harsher forms of discrimination. Research shows that many bullied individuals may become bullies themselves,

perpetuating a harmful cycle. To break this pattern, it is essential to teach our children that responding to hate with more hate only perpetuates the cycle of violence and discrimination. Instead, emphasise the importance of love and empathy in resolving conflicts and fostering positive relationships. By promoting understanding and compassion, we can work towards creating a more inclusive and harmonious society. Remember, kindness is the most powerful antidote to hate.

2. **Cultivate Cultural Understanding and Acceptance**

   Educate your children about your cultural and religious heritage and explain the significance behind your family's traditions and practices. It is important for them to understand their roots and the values that have been passed down through generations. However, it is also important to emphasise that cultural and religious identity should never be a source of shame or superiority. True tolerance means embracing diversity and respecting the beliefs and customs of others, even if they differ from our own. Encourage your children to take pride in their cultural background while remaining open-minded and respectful towards people of other backgrounds. By fostering a spirit of inclusivity and acceptance, we can cultivate a more harmonious and interconnected society. Remember, diversity is what makes our world beautiful.

3. **Nurture Open-Mindedness**

   Teach your children that identity and behaviour are not fixed, but rather choices that can evolve over time. Encourage them to explore different perspectives and challenge rigid beliefs. It is crucial to shield them from fundamentalist ideologies that promote narrow-mindedness and intolerance. Instead, foster an environment where ideas are fluid and open to discussion. Just as a growth mindset nurtures intellectual and personal development, embracing flexibility in all aspects of life promotes holistic growth. By instilling a sense of liberation and open-mindedness, we empower our children to navigate the complexities of the world with confidence and empathy. Remember, true growth encompasses every facet of our being, not just the ones that conform to our comfort zones.

4. **Promote Discernment**

   Teach your children the art of being selective when it comes to choosing their battles. Help them understand that not every conflict requires their active participation, and not every disagreement needs to end in victory. Sometimes, the wisest choice is to let go and move forward without feeling the need to justify or explain oneself. By embracing the power of letting things be, children learn the invaluable skill of prioritising their mental and emotional well-being over the need to always be right or to always have the last word. Remember, the true victory often lies in knowing when to step back and choose peace over pride.

5. **Foster Self- Esteem and Confidence**

   Nurture your child's self-esteem by fostering confidence in their own skin. Help them understand the distinction between inherent traits, like skin colour and eye colour, and optional choices. Encourage pride in their natural attributes while guiding them to make thoughtful decisions about aspects within their control. By instilling this awareness, you empower your child to embrace their unique qualities while making informed choices that align with their values and aspirations. This approach cultivates a deep sense of self-worth rooted in authenticity and self-awareness. Additionally, it equips them with the resilience to navigate societal pressures and embrace diversity, fostering a mindset of acceptance and celebration of both individual differences and shared humanity.

6. **Empowering Your Child to Confront Bullying**

   Equip your child with the tools to confront bullying situations confidently. Acknowledge their feelings and validate their experiences and emphasise that it is okay to feel upset or hurt. Then, empower them with effective strategies for responding to bullies, such as assertive comebacks and seeking support from trusted individuals. Encourage open communication about their encounters, discussing the appropriate times to seek assistance and when they can handle the situation independently. By providing guidance on navigating bullying scenarios, you help your child develop resilience and assertiveness while fostering a sense of agency over their well-being.

7. **Instil Values of Respect and Kindness**

   Uphold the golden rule: treat others as you wish to be treated. Remind your child that respect and kindness are reciprocal and that they form the foundation of positive interactions both personally and within society. By instilling these values, you equip your child to navigate relationships with empathy, understanding, and respect, fostering harmonious connections. Remember, by fostering these qualities within your child, you cultivate a legacy of empathy and kindness that extends far beyond individual interactions, shaping a brighter future for society as a whole.

8. **Manage Media Influence**

Exercise vigilance over the media your child consumes, as it significantly influences their perceptions and beliefs. In a media landscape saturated with narratives glorifying revenge, hyper-masculinity, and unrealistic beauty standards, it is crucial to be mindful of the content your child encounters. From movies portraying young protagonists seeking vengeance to unrealistic transformations shaping societal ideals, media often perpetuates harmful stereotypes and behaviours. While it may be impossible to shield your child from all objectionable content, take an active role in discussing and critiquing media messages with them. Encourage critical thinking and practicality by helping them understand the difference between fantasy and reality. By promoting a healthy scepticism and awareness of media biases, you equip your child with the tools to engage with media responsibly.

Chapter 9

Sexual Abuse

A review paper titled 'Child Sexual Abuse in India: A Systematic Review,' published in the prestigious scientific journal PlosOne, outlines the definition of Child Sexual Abuse (CSA) by the World Health Organisation (WHO). According to WHO, CSA involves a child in sexual activities beyond their comprehension, ability to give consent, or developmental readiness, which, in turn, violates societal norms and laws. These activities encompass a range, from fondling to engaging children in prostitution, pornography, or online exploitation by cyber-predators.

The alarming headline from a 12 January 2020 *India Today* article, '109 Children Sexually Abused Every Day in India in 2018: NCRB,' highlights the grim reality. However, these figures likely represent only a fraction of the actual cases, as many instances of abuse go unreported. India holds the unfortunate distinction of having the highest number of sexually abused children globally, yet there persists a pervasive reluctance to openly address this issue.

So, how can we better equip ourselves to protect our children from such abuse? The first step is to gain a deeper understanding of the causes and factors contributing to child sexual abuse, as well as debunking common myths surrounding the issue. By shedding light on these misconceptions and addressing them head-on, we can create a more informed and proactive approach to safeguarding our children.

Dr James Cantor, of the Centre for Addiction and Mental Health in Toronto, Canada was surrounded in controversy when he said that paedophilia is something that one is essentially born with, does not appear to change over time and it's as core to our being as any other sexual orientation is. He based his hypothesis on the reports of MRI scans of paedophiles done in his lab. He found that the brains of the paedophiles he studied were wired differently from non-paedophiles. The brain wiring is messed up and when it perceives a child it triggers the sexual instincts instead of triggering the nurturing instincts. However, scanning all adults in society may not be a practical approach to prevent child sexual abuse. That is why most countries try to nab paedophiles by tracking individuals who access child pornography, who have histories of other sex offences etc. But considering that most child sexual offenders are within the home, the duty of parents becomes paramount in preventing this abuse. It would be detrimental to all law enforcement if parents do not report these cases and live under the false pretence that the member abusing their child will stop his/her ways. We have just learnt that the brain wiring is different in paedophiles, and it is not going to change by keeping the abuse secret or unreported. The children suffering abuse undergo brain changes themselves that alter their lives forever. These changes (in brain anatomy, emotions or psychology) are as severe as seen in patients with post traumatic stress disorders. No wonder child sexual abuse is termed as the 'wound that time does not heal.' Therefore, to put it simply, prevention is the only cure to CSA.

There is also evidence that CSA, particularly if repeated, evokes a cascade of neurohumoral and neurotransmitter effects that produce enduring deleterious alterations in brain structure and function (Frodl et al., 2010). The brain regions affected are the hippocampus (involved in memory), amygdala (involved in emotions, depression, emotional memory, and flight-fight fear responses), corpus callosum, cerebral cortex (especially the somatosensory cortex that is involved in processing sensory inputs like touch, pain, or genital arousal) and cerebellar vermis (Rinne-Albers et al., 2013). These structural changes spell out increased risks for temperamental problems, poor social adjustment, lack of trust, insecure relations with parents, unstable relations with future partners and lower academic performance. Overall, CSA victims just become numb to emotions, relations, and senses. Other studies also indicate that people who have been through childhood abuse or neglect have a higher risk of substance abuse and obesity if they go down that path because they have a harder time controlling their urges and making rational decisions due to actual physical changes in their brain development.

Another socio-cultural factor in child sexual abuse is family secrecy. In India, the business of the family stays in the family, especially with regard to any actions that are considered inappropriate or taboo. This is because in India there are cultural elements of blame and shame (including in family systems), and families will go to great lengths to protect the reputation of the family in the community. It is also not unusual for children to be blamed for their own abuse because the rights and statements of adults tend to trump those of children. Moreover, since the child's identity is rooted in the family's identity and standing in the community, anything that would embarrass the family or tarnish their good name is kept private—in some cases even from other immediate or extended family members. This practice of secrecy only serves to protect the sexual perpetrator and allows the cycle of abuse to continue. In addition, the parents' or caregivers' refusal to believe the child victim about the sexual abuse or cover it up further exacerbates the child's distress (i.e., betrayal trauma) and prevents her or him from getting therapeutic help when needed.

Additionally, myths and taboos surrounding CSA further perpetuate silence and hinder efforts to combat this pervasive evil. Thus, it is imperative to break the silence, shed light on the prevalence of child sexual abuse, and work towards creating a society where children are protected and supported in speaking out against such atrocities.

- **Myth 1: Boys Don't Get Abused**

In his paper 'Sexual Abuse of Children and Youth in India: An Anthropological Perspective,' Dr Carson and his team found that young boys in India have a similar and sometimes higher prevalence of child sexual abuse than girls. However, patriarchal society and existing social norms around masculinity and focus on young girls as primary targets for child sexual abuse programs leave the vulnerabilities of young boys unattended and under-reported.

- **Myth 2: Child Sexual Abuse Is Limited to Underprivileged Families**

Though the incidence and probability of child sexual abuse is significantly higher in families with poor socioeconomic backgrounds, this evil is rampant across all economic statuses. The affluent usually do not report it or buy their way out due to fear of social ostracisation. A 2006 article in *Boston Daily,* 'Poor Little Rich Kids' talked about how social workers reported extreme resistance in cases of child abuse amongst the wealthy. Threats like 'I have friends in powerful places' or offering bribes to the law enforcement and/or social workers were deemed very common to avoid news of sexual abuse of their kids.

- **Myth 3: Child Abuse Happens in the West, Not in Indian Families**

Despite common misconceptions, the reality of child sexual abuse in India is stark. According to a report by BBC in September 2017:

- A child under 16 is raped every 155 minutes, with one under 10 being victimised every 13 hours.
- More than 10,000 children were raped in 2015 alone.
- A government study found that 53.22 per cent of participating children reported some form of sexual abuse.

These harrowing statistics debunk any notion that India is immune to the scourge of child sexual abuse and emphasise the urgent need for widespread awareness, prevention, and intervention efforts.

- **Myth 4: Keeping Children Away from Strangers Is Sufficient**

Contrary to popular belief, simply keeping children away from strangers does not ensure their safety from sexual abuse. Shockingly, UNICEF India reports that 50 per cent of child offenders are individuals known to the child, often within their own family or social circle. This unsettling reality highlights the urgent need for comprehensive education on personal boundaries and consent, regardless of familiarity with the perpetrator.

- **Myth 5: Family Honor Comes before the Child**

As mentioned earlier, the sanctity of the Indian family unit often leads to a culture of secrecy, where incidents deemed inappropriate or taboo are shielded from public scrutiny. Driven by the fear of societal judgement and shame, families will often prioritise preserving their reputation over addressing internal issues, even at the expense of confronting instances of child sexual abuse. This 'What will people say' attitude crosses the boundaries of financial and educational status too. This phenomenon has been reported in a statistical survey that showed that one in four families do not come out and report child sexual abuse.

Effective Strategies for Parents

1. **Good-Touch Bad-Touch Talk**

   Kids as early as 2 years should have an understanding of what parts of their bodies are private, what is a good-touch and bad-touch, and who all are allowed to touch their private parts (mom, nanny, or whoever is the primary caregiver and gives them a bath or cleans them). Also, in the talk, tell them about who are the designated safe adults they can report to in case they feel that they have been touched in their private places. Yes, it might mean a frantic call from the preschool saying that your child is not letting the school didi clean her bottom after potty (a true incident), but it means preventing a lot of trouble for your little one in the future.

2. **No Secrets or Photos**

   Tell your kids, even if they are young toddlers that no one can take photos of them without their consent. Also, if someone (no matter how well they know them) tells them a 'secret' which is not to be told to the parents, they should treat it as a red flag and report it to their designated safe adults right away.

3. **Avoid Using Derogatory Terms for Genitals**

   A huge psychological impact on young developing kids is when they are taught to call their genitals by shameful names (calling vagina or penis as 'chi chi' which means 'bad') or giving any impression to them that their genitals are negative or shameful features only makes them easier to victimise. Child sexual abusers have been many times known to lure a child by offering them cures for their 'chi chi.'

4. **Respect Your Child's Comprehension of Love, Body, and Relationships**

   If a child of 5 years says she is in love with a boy in her class, it doesn't imply that she means it in adult terms of relationships. Nor does it mean that she understands what love is. Instead, she means it in the most unconditional purest form that she is simply fond of this boy in her class. Therefore, it is up to us how we spell out love for her. Laughing it out or scolding—both are extreme approaches for this behaviour. Kids feel insulted if you laugh out their feelings. They feel belittled. Nor are they expecting to be scolded. They feel shocked if their parents say, 'Don't talk to a boy like this!' They really don't know why, and that love means physical, emotional, and mental commitment. For them, it is a new word in their dictionary as much as any other new word is. So, if your 5-year-old declares that she wants to marry a boy in her class, just keep a poker face and keep listening to what she has to say. She doesn't have to be given a lesson in marriage and sexual conduct at the age of 5! So just let it be.

5. Look Out for Red Flags

Sometimes kids do not know what is innocent and what might be a red flag. Many parents will vouch for the fact that their kids play 'mom-dad' games and have even told their friends that love is about kissing on the lips or touching private parts. Kids have a host of information and channels right in front of them. A kissing scene in a movie you might be watching or an intimate action in some song video perks up their curiosity and imagination. Thus, it is best to have age-appropriate talks about relationships and body parts with your kids. A kid of 3 years should know what are his/her private parts that no one should touch. And if anyone does, then who he/she should report it to. A kid of 5 years should know that people in love do stay together or get married. A kid of 10 should surely know that love involves both emotional and physical aspects. It is stupid to live in a bubble and think that a 10-year-old needs to know nothing. You can go on the internet or talk to a gynae friend of yours and you shall be shocked about the rise in teenage pregnancies in India. And I am talking about girls as young as 12 years. So, it is best to educate both our boys and girls about love, relationships, sex, and consent as per their age.

6. Have the Sex Talk

It is always better that you talk to your child about sex and give them correct information, before anyone else does. If you have a pre-teen in your house and you haven't had a talk about sex, then please drop everything and sit down with them. This is different from the good-touch bad-touch talk. That talk should happen as early as the young toddler stage. When your child is about to hit puberty, you should have a talk involving how and why their body is changing, what feelings they can expect for the opposite sex, and what is the safest way to approach these new changes and feelings. It is difficult to drop all taboos and talk to your kids about sex, but if you don't, then they shall get their information from some other unsolicited source, and that can never be good.

7. Update Your Ideas About Sex

We all have stories of love, crushes, romances, dates, and holding hands or kissing in our teenage or college lives. We might have even ended up living in or marrying the person we fell in love with. Then why do our kids have to be held to an impractical standard of morals and ethics? We must acknowledge that our children, like all humans, experience emotions. It is our responsibility to guide them on navigating relationships, love, and intimacy. While experiencing love is natural, engaging in casual relationships may have consequences. It is important to convey these messages to your children in a supportive and non-judgemental manner.

Practical Tips to Safeguard Your Children

1. **Don't Live in a Bubble**

   In this modern age, we often believe we understand our children completely and that they are the best. However, with societal norms constantly shifting and moral boundaries blurring, it is crucial to recognise that our children are influenced by factors beyond our control. They may be influenced more by external forces than by our guidance. While it is important to trust our children, we mustn't be naive to the possibility that they could be exposed to harmful influences. Avoid the trap of thinking, 'It can't happen to us,' or 'My child would never do that.' It is essential to remain vigilant and aware of the challenges our children face in today's complex world.

2. **Treat Your Child's Talks about Relationships and Sex Seriously**

   Children as young as five years old often begin to express curiosity about topics such as the opposite sex, marriage, and how babies are born. When they bring up these subjects, it is important not to dismiss or mock their inquiries. Instead, take them seriously and view them as a valuable opportunity to understand what your child's developing mind is processing regarding these complex matters. Engaging in open and honest conversations can help foster trust and strengthen your bond with your child. By listening attentively and providing age-appropriate information, you can support their natural curiosity and help them navigate the complexities of the world around them.

3. **Open Your Horizons Regarding Relationships and Sex**

   Ensuring your child's happiness and well-being is paramount. When having the sex talk with your child, it is not just about breaking down mental barriers around discussing sex; it also involves expanding your understanding of sexuality. Topics like same-sex relationships, premarital sex, and practising safe sex should all be part of the conversation. Ultimately, the message you want to convey is that your child's feelings, questions, and concerns are valued and respected above all else. By approaching the discussion with openness, empathy, and a focus on your child's needs, you can foster a supportive environment where they feel comfortable exploring these important aspects of their identity and relationships.

4. **Compose a Body Song for Your Toddler**

   Introducing positive body image and discussing good and bad touch from a young age is crucial. One effective method is incorporating it into everyday activities, such as singing a body song while assisting your child in bathing, starting as early as 2 years old. This not only establishes a comfortable environment for discussing these topics but also reinforces important concepts in a way that resonates with your child's daily experiences. By integrating such conversations into routine activities, you can instil a strong foundation of body positivity and safety awareness from an early age.

5. **Establish a Safety Code**

   In case of an emergency, it is important for children to have a discreet way to signal for help. Establishing a code sentence, such as 'I want a soda pop,' can serve as a covert distress signal. This code should be something unique to your family, known only to you and your child. By using a seemingly innocent phrase, your child can convey their need for assistance without alerting others. It is essential to ensure that even household staff are unaware of this code, maintaining its effectiveness as a discreet means of communication. This proactive approach equips your child with a reliable method to reach out for help in critical situations and provides both you and your child with peace of mind.

6. **Leverage Technology to Your Benefit**

   In today's digital age, leveraging safety and tracking apps can provide an added layer of security for your child. Consider utilising these technological tools to enhance your child's safety. There are various apps available that enable real-time tracking of your child's location via their cell phone. Additionally, specialised watches equipped with SOS call features offer peace of mind when your child is out and about. Many smartphones also feature an emergency dialling function, which can be activated by pressing the power button multiple times and directly connecting to emergency services. It is also advisable to equip both you and your child with a few of these safety tech solutions. Moreover, if your child spends extended periods alone at home, installing a webcam with live streaming capabilities accessible via your phone can offer added reassurance. By embracing these technological innovations, you empower yourself and your child with proactive measures to ensure their safety and well-being.

7. **Avoid Always Being Overly Virtuous**

Certainly, the perspectives on sex and celibacy have evolved significantly since our generation. Continuously dwelling on outdated norms and practices can create a communication barrier between us and our children. No one enjoys conversing with a moral authority figure. To truly connect with our children and foster open dialogue, we must adapt our understanding of sex and broaden our perspectives. Embracing a more contemporary approach to discussions about sex allows us to establish a trusting and supportive relationship with our children. By being receptive to new ideas and perspectives, we can effectively serve as trusted confidants for our children as they navigate the complexities of sexuality and relationships.

Acknowledgements

Life has come a long way since I penned my initial book with Hay House India titled *100 Ways to Be a Stress-Free Mom and Raise Happy Kids* in 2018, and the one you are currently holding in your hand, *Beyond Baby Steps.* While the former was filled with concise, two-page tips drawn from my personal experiences, *Beyond Baby Steps* is a more profound exploration, rooted in scientific research stemming from my background as a developmental neuroscientist. Both books hold a special place in my heart, each representing distinct phases and perspectives of my life's journey.

Between *100 Ways to Be a Stress-Free Mom and Raise Happy Kids* and *Beyond Baby Steps,* numerous significant milestones and life-altering events unfolded. The onset of the Covid-19 pandemic dramatically reshaped the world and our lives, requiring us to adapt to an entirely new way of living. Along this journey, we endured the heartache of losing dear friends and loved ones. Yet, despite these challenges, we emerged resilient, demonstrating the remarkable strength of the human spirit. Today, we stand with pride, a testament to the indomitable nature of the human will. Therefore, as I begin my acknowledgements, I wish to pay tribute to this unwavering spirit and offer a silent prayer for all those departed souls whose invaluable contributions can never be overstated.

The Covid-19 pandemic also catalysed a shift towards embracing science and research, marking a significant turning point in global conversations. For me, this transition felt like a homecoming, as I have always proudly embraced a scientific worldview. I attribute much of my scientific mindset and approach to the rigorous training I received at my alma mater, the Tata Institute for Fundamental Research. It was there that I honed my analytical skills and developed a deep appreciation for scientific inquiry. In particular, I am immensely grateful to my mentor, Dr Shubha Tole, whose guidance and support were instrumental in shaping my academic and professional journey. Her mentorship played a pivotal role in shaping my perspective and instilling in me a passion for scientific exploration.

Amid the challenges brought by Covid, there was a silver lining: quality family time. Despite the uncertainties, my close-knit family—comprising my husband Maninder, my daughters Parneet and Avneet, and my father-in-law affectionately called Onkar Papa—found solace in each other's company. We shared moments of pure joy, laughter, and bonding, often over spirited games of Ludo and Snakes and Ladders during the lockdown. Despite facing the impact of Covid firsthand, our family remained steadfast in prioritising what truly matters: positivity and happiness.

I express my deepest gratitude to Maninder and Onkar Papa for exemplifying unwavering support for women. Their belief in me and their encouragement to pursue a successful career based on my strengths are inspiring stories of feminism and the importance of uplifting women within the family. In moments of self-doubt, their steadfast confidence in me never wavered, serving as a beacon of inspiration and empowerment.

Maninder holds a special place in my acknowledgements for his remarkable ability to nurture the best in me with gentle sincerity. His honesty, whether in offering praise or constructive criticism, defines our relationship and makes him not just my best friend but also the most genuine life partner I could ask for. He embodies resolute support, providing both a solid foundation to lean on and a safe space to express frustrations.

My parents, Anu and Girish, and my brother, Sagar, have weathered their fair share of life's ups and downs over the past few years, both figuratively and literally—whether it's navigating life's challenges or braving the roller coasters at Six Flags in Austin. Their resilience and positivity serve as a beacon of hope, showing how one can emerge stronger and happier even in the face of adversity. Sagar, in particular, embodies the essence of gender-neutral parenting, exemplifying mental fortitude and a remarkable sense of positivity. Kudos to him for being a shining example! Arianna, my niece, is the kindest soul I know. Her genuine love for family and her radiant warmth never fail to brighten up the room. I can't wait for that summer we are planning together, my dear child!

My daughters are my greatest treasures, lighting up my world in ways I never imagined. Watching them grow into strong, independent young women fills me with immense pride. Despite the challenges of this era, they demonstrate respect and sound judgement. Girls, my hope for you is to continue thriving, prioritising your well-being, and staying true to your passions in life. Know that my love for you knows no bounds!

It is often said that the company you keep shapes who you are. In my life, I am fortunate to be surrounded by a diverse and incredible group of friends who have left an indelible mark on my journey. Pathika, you are the epitome of uniqueness, a one-of-a-kind soul. Dr Ananta and Dr Neha, here is to our everlasting girls' weekends, defying time and distance. Poorva, Gauri, Kanchan, and Sharika, our bond has left a lasting impression on the universe, and we are just getting started. And to those who have joined my circle later in life, like Kajal, Surbhi, Bhawna, Nupur, Dr Rajat, Dev, Ajay, Hasmukh, Shipra, Daniel, and Amanpreet, your presence has enriched my life beyond measure. Here is to many more adventures together!

My acknowledgements won't be complete if I don't give a shout-out to all those who doubted me, ridiculed me, gossiped about me, or lied to me. To each of you, I extend my gratitude, for your scepticism and negativity that fuelled my determination to prove myself. You have inadvertently contributed to the person I have become, and for that, I am truly thankful.

From here on,
It's only onwards and upwards.
Life . . . here I come!

About the Author

Lahar Bhatnagar Singh is a distinguished scientific parenting coach, author, corporate trainer, and blogger specialising in contemporary urban parenting. Certified by the International Association of Certified Coaches, USA, she possesses a deep understanding of developmental neuroscience, backed by numerous international papers and research in the field. Leveraging her expertise in brain function, psychology, and evolution, she has developed workshops tailored to assist parents of young children (0-7 years) in navigating the challenges of modern-day parenting.

Under the banner of Nirvana-Ma, she endeavours to cultivate a nurturing environment conducive to happiness and stress-free living. Her vision is to empower caregivers and foster empathy, peace, and intellectual growth, thereby shaping a harmonious society for the future. With a keen focus on the Indian context and the unique challenges faced by Indian children, her work is meticulously crafted to address these concerns.

Recognised as one of India's top 30 bloggers by Momspresso, Lahar contributes articles on parenting to the prestigious *Times of India* and has been featured in various parenting platforms such as Sipping Thoughts, Firstcry, and Momspresso. She offers a wealth of meticulously researched articles aimed at guiding mothers toward happiness and equipping them with strategies for raising children to their full potential in today's world.

Lahar's repertoire includes the acclaimed book, *100 Ways to Become a Stress-Free Mom and Raise Happy Kids,* published by the renowned international publisher Hay House India. In addition to her literary contributions, Lahar conducts dynamic parenting workshops across play schools, corporates, and pre-schools, both online and offline. These scientifically designed workshops offer practical insights and tips for Indian moms to navigate the challenges of modern parenting while nurturing well-rounded, talented children. Filled with practical examples, exercises, and checklists, her workshops are engaging and effectively communicate important scientific concepts in an accessible manner.

For inquiries and consultations, to learn more about upcoming workshops, or to invite Lahar to conduct a Nirvana-Ma workshop, please email to nirvanamaa@gmail.com.

'The gateways to wisdom and knowledge are always open.'

Louise Hay